Longhorn Tales

Stories of Ranching in Colorado, New Mexico and Texas

*To James
The favorite
Grandchild*

Larry Wright

Larry Wright

DENVER, COLORADO

Longhorn Tales
Stories of Ranching in Colorado, New Mexico and Texas

Cover Photo © 2012 Virgina Wright.

Outskirts Press, Inc.
http://www.outskirtspress.com

ISBN: 978-1-4327-7948-1

Outskirts Press and the "OP" logo are trademarks belonging to Outskirts Press, Inc.

PRINTED IN THE UNITED STATES OF AMERICA

Table of Contents

Illustrations

Preface

Will James once wrote:

"To my way of thinking there's something wrong, or missing, with any person who hasn't got a soft spot in their heart for an animal of some kind…With me, my weakness lays towards the horse…To me, the horse is man's greatest, most useful, faithful, and powerful friend." James, Will. Preface. Smoky, the Cow Horse.

This sums up a lot for me. While I started a little later in life and certainly was not the horseman that Mr. James was, I always had a certain feeling for horses and tried to understand them and communicate with them. It is the basis for why I loved ranching and why I wanted to write this book.

I got my first horse, a little sorrel mare named Rose, for my eighth birthday. We could not afford a saddle, so for about a year I rode her bareback. She was well broke but had the roughest trot that I have ever experienced. At first, trying to ride Rose without a saddle was disastrous, but she always took good care of me. Whenever she got into her trot, either going up from a walk, or down from a lope, I would start to slide off of her back, sometimes slipping under her belly, and she would immediately stop and not take another step until I got up.

By the time I got my first saddle, I could ride her or any other horse bareback, regardless of the gait or circumstance. Not only could I stay on, I learned how a horse moves and to move with it. I think not having a saddle for a year was one of the best things that ever happened to me. This was the beginning of my relationship with horses and also my interest in ranching.

My Aunt-in-law, Ruth Jarboe, owned and operated the Texarkana Stockyards and whenever I could I would ride Rose to the sale barn and work cattle on her. I got to know and respect the cowboys who worked there and the ranchers who brought cattle in to sell. After awhile I was helping round up and work cattle on the nearby ranches.

I got away from horses and ranching when I went to college and worked first in Baton Rouge and then in Denver. I put up with the city for awhile, but was constantly thinking about horses and ranching. I was married to Virginia and had two young daughters, Myka and Jamie. I don't know how I convinced them that we would be better off living on a ranch, rather than in the city, but they were very willing to try. I soon realized that I could not have done it without them. It was amazing how quickly they learned and how helpful they were. It was truly a family affair.

PREFACE

Myka and Jamie soon became excellent horsewomen and Virginia was absolutely at home on the ranch and in the ranching community. A lot of the stories are about them and all of the stories were inspired by them. They were also invaluable in helping me remember and develop the details of each story. This book is dedicated to them with my thanks.

It Doesn't Get Any Better Than This

"Neighboring" in the ranching community means that if you are going to work cattle, roundup, brand, ship, etc., you can count on your neighbors to come and help with the job. This is very beneficial because you do not have to have extra cowboys on your payroll on a year round basis or hire temporary help for a particular project, which helps with the all important bottom line.

In the spirit of this camaraderie, I agreed to help Clint Hoagland, a neighbor and friend, with a roundup one February morning. When I got up that morning, at 4:00 a.m., it seemed to be pretty cold. I stoked the fire in the stove and added a couple of logs. I checked the OT (outside temperature) and it was -3 degrees. I turned on the outside light and peeked out the window. It looked like there was at least four inches of new snow on the ground. I immediately regretted my decision to neighbor on this particular day. Not having fully thought it out, I woke my wife and asked her to come up with a credible excuse as to why I couldn't go. She was not excited about being awakened. She mumbled something and rolled over and covered her head. I took this to mean that she was not willing to help out.

I decided that I really didn't have a choice. I went to the barn to catch and saddle Lusty Lu, my choice of horse for that day. Half way through saddling him I wondered why I hadn't practiced this usually simple task with gloves on. I finally got him saddled and loaded in the trailer and went back in the house to warm my hands and put on another layer of clothes.

I got to the Hoagland's house and checked on Lusty to see how he had made the cold trip. He looked like he was doing better than me so I went inside to have breakfast.

The roundup covered about thirty miles and went well except for about a twenty mph wind. By 11:30 a.m. we had the cattle moved and were heading back to the house. It had warmed up to almost -1. We were going through a stand of pines and the limbs were laden with snow. I decided I had to get even with Clint for putting me through this ordeal. I rode up beside him and waited for the opportune moment. As we approached a low hanging limb with lots of snow, I moved in front a little bit and hit the branch as I went by. It was perfect, the snow landed directly on top of him. I spurred Lusty and made the last half-mile to the house in about fifty seconds. I was sitting on the back porch by the stove when Clint walked in still covered with snow. He blustered, half mad and half laughing, "You son-of-a-bitch". I looked at the fire in the stove, smiled and said to myself, "You know, it doesn't get any better than this!"

So, I am saying to anyone who might by chance be reading this book, "If you didn't enjoy this story, don't bother reading any further because it doesn't get any better than this."

Cow Pony Race

THERE ARE SOME EVENTS IN a person's life that are special. On an August day in 1979, I experienced such an event.

I was fortunate to own one of the best overall cow horses that ever lived. His name was Lusty Lu. He could do anything and he loved doing it. He was the most feared competitor in a number of events at the annual county fairs in the area. In most of the events he was ridden by my daughter Jamie, who from age 11 was a very outstanding horsewoman. In some of the events he was ridden by me, which was a definite handicap, but Lusty never let it show.

In 1979, when Jamie was 13, the whole family attended the Elbert County Fair in Kiowa, Colorado. We looked over the program to see what all events were scheduled, and decide which ones we should enter. In the morning, there was the 4-H gymkhana. We entered Lusty and Jamie in both the barrel race and pole bending. In the afternoon, there were several events scheduled in both the arena and on the track. We entered Lusty in the quarter mile cow pony race on the track, the cowhide race in the arena, and finally the half mile cow pony race back on the track.

For those of you who are not familiar with a cow pony race or a cowhide race, I will attempt to explain. In a cow pony race, the horses are somewhat lined up facing the opposite direction that the race is to be run. When the starting gun is fired, the horses must sprint about 20 yards past a designated line and reverse direction to run the race. In addition to having the speed to win the race, the horses have to rein well and have the ability to turn around in a very tight and crowded field of horses. There is a definite advantage to being in front when you make the turn. In both the quarter mile and half mile race we had two distinct advantages. We had Jamie, who was an excellent horsewoman and absolutely fearless, and we had Lusty who was big, strong, and quick as a cat and could stop and turn on a dime. At age 13, Jamie already had two years of experience and had run in several similar races in the area.

The cowhide race is entirely different. It is a timed event in the arena. A rope is attached to a very green cowhide that smells like the offal dump at a rendering plant. A "jockey" rides the cowhide and a horse and rider pull the cowhide up the arena (about fifty yards) around a barrel and then back to the finish line.

This race presents several problems. First, you must have a jockey to ride the smelly hide and who is sober enough to stay on. Second, you have to have a horse that isn't afraid to get close enough to the fresh hide so that the rope can be attached to the saddle horn. The horse has to have the strength and stamina to pull the hide around the barrel and back across the finish line at a very fast pace. Finding a good horse for this is not an easy task. When the horse gets close to the hide and smells it, if often goes berserk and remains out of control when you start to pull the hide up the arena.

Getting back to the day's events, Jamie rode Lusty in the barrel and pole bending competition, and she finished second and third in those two events. The gymkhana events were supposed to be over by lunch time, but because of the number of entries, it was well after 1:00 p.m. before Jamie and Lusty finished.

Jamie had not even gotten back to our horse trailer to give Lusty a quick break when they called the quarter mile cow pony race. Jamie hustled Lusty to the starting line for the race, only to find that the other eleven entries had already lined up and established their positions. We had hoped for an outside position to avoid some of the chaos and confusion that always exists when the horses make the turn to start the race. Jamie, because of her late arrival, was stuck in the middle of the pack. But, as was typical with Jamie and Lusty, when they made the turn they were on top, and by the end of the quarter mile, they were ahead by six lengths.

A few minutes after the race was over on the track they called the cowhide race in the arena. At this point, I had not yet put my saddle on Lusty and did not have a "jockey" to ride the cowhide. I spotted an old friend that I thought might do it (which meant that he had probably had enough beer to disregard the smell of the hide). For a percentage of the purse, my friend agreed. The biggest problem was that he weighed about 210 lbs. which is not what you are looking for in terms of a "jockey".

I quickly took Jamie's saddle off of Lusty and put mine on. We were the thirteenth contestant in the race. When they offered me the rope to pull the hide, Lusty didn't flinch. As usual he was up to the task at hand and paid no attention to the smell of the hide. Even with a 210 lb. passenger we easily won the event.

We had just finished the pull when they announced the half-mile cow pony race. We hurriedly took my saddle off and put Jamie's back on. By this time, Lusty was getting pretty gaunt. I tightened the cinch to its normal hole, thinking it was the correct tightness. After saddling Lusty, I went to the top of the judge's stand in the arena so I could view the entire race around the track.

Jamie rushed Lusty to the starting line, which was in front of the bleachers. The track was a one-half mile oval, so the race started and finished in the same place. Jamie, again, had a difficult starting position but, again, made the best of it. She got off to a good start and soon was in the lead. She increased her lead with every stride and was eight or nine lengths in front as they came to the top of the stretch. It was then that I witnessed an amazing feat of horsemanship. Because of Lusty's gaunt condition and my careless tightening of the cinch, the saddle began slipping off of Lusty's back. As it slipped, Jamie "walked off" of the saddle and was riding Lusty bareback. When the saddle slipped all of the way under Lusty, he started crowhopping, and continued to do so until he crossed the finish line, still in front by a length.

I was scared to death, as all of the other horses in the race were crowding up to Jamie, who by this time was just trying to stay on the bucking Lusty. Keep in mind that Lusty weighed 1,150 lbs. and Jamie weighed less than 90 lbs. I virtually jumped off of the judge's stand and ran to where Jamie had stopped Lusty and gotten off. When I got to her, she was a little shook up, but not nearly as shook up as I was.

As we walked Lusty back in front of the bleachers, the crowd gave us a standing ovation. I tipped my hat to the crowd, thinking that they were applauding my leap off of the judge's stand and my dash to Jamie's side. It later occurred to me that the applause may have been for Jamie's ride and for Lusty's efforts in winning the race under some very difficult conditions.

*Jamie and Lusty (second from left)
lined up for start of Cow Pony Race*

A Little Logic Goes a Long Way

TO FULLY APPRECIATE THIS STORY, you have to know a little bit about our vet, Dr. Woodrow Smith, and a little bit about me.

Woody was 5'8" tall, weighed about 160 lbs., was strong as an ox, and was very temperamental (actually volatile) especially during calving season (January through mid-April). He was also a very good veterinarian and extremely practical. Having been raised in eastern Colorado on a cattle ranch, he knew how hard it was to make a living at ranching. Although he had a nice clinic in town, much of his practice was working out of the back of his vet truck, and being a sole practitioner, he was on call almost all the time during calving season - sometimes he even worked around the clock. I am sure the lack of sleep and long hours of dedication to his profession contributed to the bad temperament that Woody made no attempt to hide. His unpredictable foul disposition led most ranchers to avoid calling on his services during calving season unless it was absolutely necessary. But, he was always there when you needed him, and sometimes, though not often, he would be in one of his very talkative, good moods.

Now to understand me, you just need to know that I enjoy a good practical joke and that I get a kick out of poking fun when the chance arises or the mood strikes me. Some folks have even said I have a wry or dry sense of humor. It isn't always appreciated by everyone though, and one particular Saturday in March, Woody's mood and my personality crossed paths.

The encounter began when my daughter, Myka, son-in-law, Pat, and I were checking the cows in our creek bottom pasture that we used for calving, when we spotted a cow that was suffering from a serious prolapse. It appeared, the cow had discharged almost all of her uterus. She was a pretty wild cow and since it would be almost impossible to drive her back to the barn and corrals, we decided the best thing to do was to get a rope on her and hold her until we could figure out what to do next. We got her roped and tied to one of the many cottonwood trees that lined the creek. The creek bank at that point was very steep and when we snubbed her to the tree she was facing uphill with her rear end about 10 feet from the water's edge. Unfortunately, during this process, the uterus became covered with sand, so I realized that to try and reinsert the unclean uterus back into her in that condition would be a bad idea.

The sun was setting when I rode to the house and made the call to Woody for help. He was on another call but his wife said she would relay the information and get him to our place as soon as possible. I told her where on the ranch we would be, and since Woody was familiar with the ranch, I felt sure he would know how to find us. I collected a couple of flash lights, a bucket of warm water, and drove my pickup to the opposite bank of the creek about 50 ft. from where we had tied the cow, so that we could use the headlights to illuminate the "operating room".

During what turned out to be a 2 hour wait for Woody, we washed the sand off of the uterus and Pat held it in the bucket of warm water to keep it from collecting more sand. By the time Woody arrived, it was pitch dark and cold. We didn't know what kind of mood Woody was going to be in, but the three of us were certainly not in a very sociable mood. Woody pulled up next to where my pickup was parked and got the necessary items out of the back of his vet truck. He waded across the creek to where we were, not yet having said a word.

By this time the cow had quit struggling and, in fact, was fairly docile. She was snubbed pretty short to the tree and was still facing uphill when Woody viewed the situation and he actually looked rather pleased at the circumstances. Finally he said "I'm sorry to keep you waiting this long" and then spent the next fifteen minutes telling us about his previous ranch call where he had to rope and tie a heifer to his vet truck to perform a C-section on the uncooperative cow. The way he told it was very funny and Woody was having a good time entertaining us. He was on a roll and continued to amuse us with some of his other humorous experiences as he prepared to push the bulging uterus back into our cow. Woody had done this so often that it was just second nature to him, so we thought the procedure would take no more than thirty minutes.

Woody had been working on the cow for about 20 minutes and had not made much progress. He was still talking and joking with us and every time he would shove a portion of the organ in and reach for more, the portion he shoved in would come back out. I was trying to figure out if the cow was having contractions and therefore expelling the uterus, or if there was some other problem. Then I sort of figured out that because the cow was facing uphill it was logical that the problem was more one of gravity than of muscle contractions. Woody was in such a good mood I hated to say anything, but finally asked, "Woody, do you think that if we turned the cow around so that she is facing downhill, it might help?" Woody quit talking, looked at me and said, "You know, you may be right".

We loosened the rope a bit and maneuvered her around so that she was facing downhill. Sure enough, Woody had the uterus back in and the cow sewn up in less than 15 minutes. Woody was a little chagrined but still in a pretty good mood when I took a chance and asked if he would like me to ride along on his other ranch calls in order to help with some of the more technical situations that might arise. Even his stare didn't deter me from ribbing him a little further when I asked how much the job would pay.

Needless to say, Woody was no longer in a good mood.

How to Deal With
Fence Jumping Steers

THERE ARE SOME ANIMALS THAT are truly amazing. When Virginia and I ranched on the plains of eastern Colorado we had two big Longhorn steers that weighed over 1800 lbs. We kept them around mainly for show and despite their weight and massive horns that spanned 6 1/2 feet in width, the steers were fairly gentle. Amazingly, they were very quick and agile, and as I found out, could jump a five strand barbed wire fence with ease.

I never had a problem with these longhorns until one summer we were running some yearling heifers and turned the two steers in with them. This worked out okay for a couple of weeks. Then one day while checking on the heifers, I noticed the steers were missing. At first I assumed they broke through the fence, so I rode the pasture to see where they may have gotten out. The fences were good and tight and I couldn't find a hole anywhere. I was puzzled as to what had happened and thinking someone may have stolen them, I called the sheriff's office to report them missing. A week or so went by with no sign of the two steers. One day, I got a call from my neighbor who let me know the two runaways were in with some of his cows.

I figured I could get them in by myself, so the next morning I saddled Lusty and went looking. It didn't take long. I found them about two miles from my pasture in the middle of my neighbor's cows. I cut them out and headed them back home. They drove well enough until I pushed them through the gate into my pasture. I got off Lusty to close the gate and as I was getting back on, the two steers made a little circle around me and jumped the fence we had just come through. By the time I got the gate open and back on Lusty, they were disappearing over a hill, heading back to their adopted mother cows.

Colorado Longhorns

Colorado Longhorns

I found them again in the midst of the cows, and repeated my earlier routine. This time I got them through the home gate, and pushed them about a quarter of a mile into the pasture to keep them from doubling back on me. I hustled back on Lusty to close the gate, but before I could get it closed, the two steers came running, jumped the fence like two buck deer, and headed back to what they now considered home. It was getting late and both Lusty and I were tired, so I decided to call it a day.

That night I called my neighbor and told him about my predicament. He said the steers were not bothering anything and I could leave them with his cows. I thanked him profusely, and offered to pay the going rate for pasture.

This worked out pretty well for the summer, but as fall approached, my neighbor started feeding his cows. A couple of weeks into his feeding season, he called me and said I would have to come get my steers, because whenever he would put feed into the two feed troughs in the pasture, the longhorns would take up a position at each of the troughs and use their horns to keep his cows from eating.

I rode out the next morning to look over the situation and to figure out how best to handle the problem. This time when I approached the herd, the two wily steers immediately took off to the far end of the pasture. I could see that getting them back home was no longer going to be a one man job.

The next day I rounded up a four man posse of friends and family and set out to bring the outlaw steers in, dead or alive. I cautioned my posse to keep between the steers and any fence they could potentially jump. By this time I had decided my two show steers were much more trouble than they were worth, and that if and when I got them penned, I would feed them corn for two or three months and hopefully, that would be enough fattening time to result in tender ribeyes, T-bones and tenderloins. The rest I determined would make good hamburger meat.

With some difficulty, we were able to drive the steers back to the barn, but knowing their agility and propensity to clear five strand wire fences at will, I figured the only pen I had that would keep them in was our seven foot high stallion pen. We got them in the pen and I threw them some hay to keep them happy until I could get into town to pick up some feed. That next morning when I checked on them, to my surprise, there was only one steer in the pen. It was obvious what had happened since the seven foot metal gate to the pen was crushed down about two feet.

Again, I had a decision to make – should I get my 30-30 and go hunting, or should I make one more attempt to gather the offender? Even though it was logical to think the missing steer had gone back to his beloved cows, I wasn't sure, but knew the remaining steer would know where to find his pal, so I rounded up my posse and turned the remaining steer out. He immediately jumped my fence, as he had before, and headed straight for the neighbor's cows. Sure enough, the other steer was there waiting for him, and for us.

By this time the longhorns had enough experience to know what was coming, so even with the posse, it was no easy task to bring the steers back. We finally got them in the barn and I locked the doors to hopefully prevent any further escape.

Now it was time to put this matter of the wandering steers behind me. My friend who ran a locker plant in town and had processed beef for us in the past was my first call. Normally you had to have an appointment at least two weeks in advance to take something in for processing. I explained my dilemma and prevailed upon our friendship to allow me to bring the two steers in the next day. Since they were not going to be "corn" fed, as I had planned, I told him I wanted to put everything into hamburger meat.

A couple of weeks later my friend called to tell me my meat was ready, and that if I wanted to pick it all up in one trip, I should bring a big truck. When I got to the plant, he told me that the total yield of meat came to over 2,100 lbs. I thought for a minute and asked to borrow his calculator and after doing a little computing, I said to him, "You mean that if I eat three lbs. of hamburger meat a day, every day, for two years, I might eventually eat it all?" He replied, "That's about it."

As it turned out there were some good things about this little episode. First, because the hamburger meat included all the good cuts - steaks and roasts, etc., - it was excellent. Second, over the next several months, we gave hamburger away, we had big hamburger parties and we learned several new ways to use hamburger helper. We eventually got through it all, and enjoyed it. And finally, we had two nice longhorn heads to hang in our barn and two nice cowhide rugs for the house.

There's no way I would want to go through it all again, but if I do, I will come to the conclusion much sooner that fence jumping steers make good hamburger meat!

My Border Collie Is Smarter Than Your Honor Student, Bandit, The Wonder Puppy

I HAVE NEVER BEEN A FAN of bumper stickers and I have never put one on any of my vehicles. However, there have been occasions when I wish I had. That's when a soccer mom or dad passes me and the bumper sticker on the back bumper of the Cadillac Escalade reads, "My Son Is An Honor Student". That's when I wish I had in place the only bumper sticker I ever liked, "My Border Collie Is Smarter Than Your Honor Student". If I had, I would have passed the Escalade so that the driver could see and know my sentiments. I guess the reason I like that bumper sticker so much is because it is one of the few that is actually true.

My first encounter with a Border Collie was when one showed up at our ranch in Colorado. I didn't know whether it was a stray that someone had dropped off or belonged to someone that would want him back. He was a good looking dog and looked well cared for. He didn't look like the typical stray. I passed the word around to my neighbors that I had him and put up a notice at the local feed store. I already had two dogs, (who were not cow dogs) and I really didn't want another one. A couple of days went by and I had not heard anything about a lost dog.

On the third day I had to gather some cows and set out on horseback to get them, leaving the three dogs at the house. I had arranged the gates to the corrals in such a way that I could easily pen the cows. As I approached the pens and barn with the cows, I was joined by the stray. He promptly positioned himself in the vicinity of the gate and began working the cows back toward me. I yelled at him to get out of the way, but that seemed to make him work even harder, doing his best to bring the cows to me. I soon realized that my cows were not "dog broke" as they scattered in all directions. I was mad and I said to myself, "I thought Border Collies were supposed to be good working dogs." I chased him back to the house and went out to regather the cows. As I approached the pens the same thing happened again. He positioned himself at the gate and seemed determined to drive the cows over me rather than let them through the gate. This time I got off my horse and locked him in the barn and went out to round the cows up for a third time.

Later that night I was talking on the phone with a friend of mine about the day's events, and how stupid this "supposed" cow dog was. He said that he had not had much experience with Border Collies, but he had heard that their instinct was to gather cattle not drive them. This did not do much to cool me off, but the next day I went to the local library and checked out a couple of books on the breed. Sure enough, my friend was right. They can be trained to drive cattle but generally they think their job is to gather them and bring them to you.

I really didn't know what I was doing, but the next day I decided to experiment a little. I got the collie in hand and turned the penned cattle out. Having been penned up for two days they moved out at a pretty good pace. I let them get about a quarter of a mile out in the pasture and I told the dog. "Okay, go get 'em, bring them in" and to my dismay he did just that. He caught up with them, circled them a couple of times and in a few minutes, had them turned around and headed back to the barn. By the time he got them through the gate those cows were "dog broke". I waited a few minutes to see if he would also close the gate, and in his own way, he did. He laid down in the middle of the opening and stared intently at the herd of cows. If one came close to the gate, he would stand up and glare at it, and the cow would retreat back to the herd. I watched for awhile and I believe he would have stayed there forever had I not relieved him by closing the gate.

Over the next couple of days, I had my new dog gather cows and move them from one pasture to another. Even though this was not a necessary chore at the time, I did it just so I could watch him work. I was really getting to like this little stray.

Then I got a phone call and the caller asked me if I was

the one that had found a Border Collie. I wanted to tell him "No" but decided it best to be honest about it. When he came to pick up his dog it was evident that they knew each other. Apparently he had lost him while looking at some cows my neighbor had for sale.

By this time I was determined to get me a Border Collie of my own. I looked through the Denver Post want ads for a few days and found an ad, "Free to a good home, six month old registered Border Collie." I called the number in the paper and the woman that answered the phone described the puppy "Bandit" and said that she and her husband really loved him but he was a little too nervous and high strung. Virginia and I decided to drive the 75 miles to Arvada, to check him out.

Bandit's then home was located in a typical suburban neighborhood with houses too close together and small yards. His owners were very nice but seemed a little suspicious of Virginia and me. They introduced us to Bandit who was in a very small back yard. He was absolutely beautiful, very friendly and good natured. It was obvious why they had named him Bandit. He had a dark patch over his right eye. His owners told us that his main problem was that whenever they had the water sprinkler on, he would circle it continuously. I convinced myself that this was not a problem and all Bandit wanted to do was work. "Herding" the sprinkler was his only outlet to do what he was bred to do.

We decided that we would take him and didn't figure that there would be any problem, but when we told the owners that we wanted him, they said, "Not so fast, we have to check you out first". They said they would bring Bandit out to the ranch the next weekend and, if they approved of where he would be living, then we could have him. I was livid and told them we were taking him home that night or not at all, and if they wanted to come visit him at the ranch, they could come anytime. They finally decided that it would be okay for us to have him.

Then they told us that Bandit had only ridden in a car twice, once when they bought him and brought him home and once when they took him to the vet to be castrated. We realized that this was a problem when we tried to get him in the truck. We finally got him loaded and Virginia cradled him in her arms all the way home. We had planned to have dinner in Denver but decided against it. It was pretty late when we got home, and when we let him out of the truck he was amazed at the wide open spaces, a far cry from the small back yard at his previous residence.

When we got in the house there were four messages on our answering machine all of them from the previous owners, asking us how he had made the trip. I called them back and assured them that everything went ok and invited them to come to the ranch to visit Bandit any time. They called a couple of more times to check on Bandit but never came to the ranch. I finally had me a genuine Border Collie.

Bandit, the wonder puppy

Bandit settled into his new home and life pretty quick. It was the middle of November and every day we were feeding hay to the cows we had in the creek bottom awaiting calving. Before we got Bandit, I would load the hay in the back of the pickup and take it to the cows by myself. After getting Bandit I wanted him to go with me and get used to cows. At first, since he was still reluctant to ride in the truck, Virginia would go with us and comfort him along the way. When we would get to the creek bottom pasture, we would go through the gate and start honking the horn to call the cows. The first day when we went through the gate, we let Bandit out. He followed very close to the truck and as the cows began to come in he was somewhat intimidated. This is the first time he had ever seen a cow or, for that matter, anything that big. However, as the cows stopped and started eating the hay that had been dumped out he sat down beside the truck to ponder the situation. In a few minutes he started edging his way toward the cows. He would go a little ways and crouch down flat against the ground. He would look the situation over carefully. Then, he would go a little farther and do the same thing. After a few minutes, when he got close to the herd, he started circling them to gather them into a tight bunch.

After that, during subsequent feedings, Bandit did not wait for the cows to get to the hay. As soon as we let him out of the truck he would start looking for them and commence driving them toward us. This did not require a lot of effort or expertise on Bandit's part because the cows were eager to get to the hay, but it did a lot for his confidence and it also helped "dog break" the cows.

Even though Bandit was feeling pretty proud of himself, he did encounter one major problem that he could not overcome. We had a rogue cow elk that hung out with the cows. She would always stand off about 50 yards away as I was putting out the hay. Then when I would drive away she would join the cows and eat with them. Bandit could not figure out why this strange looking cow did not come in with the rest of the herd. He would go after her and try to bring her in, but being somewhat more agile than the normal cow, she would evade him and out circle him. Sometime she would make a run at him and this further confused him. He could easily avoid a normal cow's charge, but this rogue would come pretty close to getting him. Bandit finally decided that being 99% successful in bringing the cows in was good enough and left the elk alone.

We had gone through this feeding routine for a couple of weeks and Bandit was not only getting over his reluctance to ride in the truck, he was eager to go. As I would load the hay he would sit by the door of the truck anxious to get in.

In order to get to the creek bottom pasture we had to go through our alfalfa field. One day, as we went through the hayfield, there were about a dozen cows grazing on the left over alfalfa sprouts. I drove through them thinking that they would follow the truck back to the pasture. Apparently they decided that the alfalfa sprouts were better than the hay. There was no indication that I could lead them to what they considered less than "greener pastures". I knew that it would be futile to try to drive them on foot. (If God had wanted you to work cattle on foot, he wouldn't have made the horse). I figured that the only way to get them off the alfalfa was to go back to the house, catch and saddle a horse and drive them back to their pasture. This was not a particularly attractive solution as the temperature was about 20° and the wind chill was probably about 10.

I was thinking about what other options I had. We were sitting in the middle of the cows and Bandit was whining in anticipation looking at the cows through the truck window. Since I really didn't want to go with my first idea (getting a horse, etc.), I decided to see what my 6 ½ month old puppy could do. I drove to the gate that led into the creek bottom and found out how the cows got out. They had knocked the gate down. I drove through the gate a little ways. I didn't want to honk the horn because I was afraid of attracting the

other cows. I certainly didn't want the whole herd in the hay
field. I let Bandit out and pointed to the errant cows in the
hayfield and said "go get 'em, bring them in". The cows were
scattered over a pretty wide area and because of the alfalfa
sprouts, were not the least bit interested in being rounded up.
Bandit circled them several times, and eventually got them
in a pretty tight bunch. He then began to push them toward
the gate and where I had parked the truck. In a few minutes
the "wonder puppy" had them through the gate and up to
the truck. Now I ask you, could your honor student do that?

The next day I advertised my saddle horses for sale.

0 to 40 in 1.2 Seconds

IN QUARTER HORSE RACING, THE break from the gate is most important. A Quarter Horse can achieve full speed in three strides and can run a quarter of a mile in 21 seconds. This translates into 42 mph. While the break from the gate in a quarter horse race is very important, I found out just how important it is from an entirely different standpoint, as you will see.

We owned a very promising two year old colt, by the name of "Go Top Copy" that we entered in the Colorado State Fair futurity at a cost of about $2,000.00. Because of the number of horses paid up in the futurity, there were five trial races. The ten fastest times in the trials would qualify for the finals.

Two important ingredients of getting a two year old colt ready for his first race are conditioning and gate training. I had decided early on that my daughter, Jamie, and I would break Copy and condition him for the race. After breaking him to ride, Jamie was in charge of conditioning and I was in charge of the gate training. Jamie at 14 had already ridden many match races and was adept at riding a racing saddle. She did most of the conditioning work in her racing saddle while I did all of the gate work in a western saddle.

At our ranch we had a three horse starting gate and I would work Copy almost daily around and in them. I stood him in the gates without a saddle and led him through them until he felt comfortable just being around them. Then I rode him in and through the gates again and again. Gradually I worked him out of the gates as they opened - slowly at first, then at full speed.

Before a young horse is allowed to compete on an official track, it has to go through what is called a "schooling" process. An owner or trainer is required to take their entry to the track and, under the supervision of the track stewards, load him in the gates with another horse. When the gates are opened, the two horses then compete in a short sprint down the track. The stewards observe how the horse acts while being loaded and how straight he runs down the track. If the horse wasn't sufficiently trained, the stewards had the authority to not allow him to race until he went through the process again and they were satisfied that he was ready. I felt comfortable with the progress Copy had made as far as how he would load into the gate and break from it, but was a little concerned about how he would behave competing against another horse. I scheduled Copy's schooling race for the weekend before the futurity trials, hoping that if he did not pass the first time, I would have enough time during the week to work out any problems.

I wanted to put Copy through a practice run before his official schooling race. To do this, I needed a few things - a track, a rider, and another horse for him to compete against. I got permission from the El Paso County Fair Board to use the track at their fair grounds and lined up my veterinarian's assistant, an ex-jockey, to ride Copy. I figured Jamie could ride one of our retired race horses, Lusty Lu. Since Jamie had ridden Lusty in several match races, I knew that he was dependable and would be a safe trip for her. I wasn't that sure about Copy, so I did not want her to be the one on him.

We set up this trial run one week before the official schooling race was to be held. Our assistant vet (jockey) was to meet us at the fairgrounds at six p.m. Jamie, Virginia, a couple of friends and I arrived at about five. I saddled Copy while Jamie saddled Lusty. Everyone was nervous, especially me. Six o'clock came and went with no sign of our practice jockey. Now I was really getting nervous. Seven o'clock came and still nothing. Because of who he worked for and how busy they always were at the clinic, we figured he got tied up in an emergency. It was starting to get dark and I was getting desperate. I very reluctantly came to the conclusion that if we were going to get anything accomplished that night we were going to have to find a substitute rider. I looked around and there were only the five of us, my wife, our two friends that had never been on a horse, Jamie who was going to ride Lusty, and me. The "and me" was what concerned me the most.

I had never ridden in a racing saddle before and I didn't want to start that evening. I talked the situation over with Jamie and Virginia. Jamie, of course, was willing to ride Copy, but if she did, who would ride Lusty. Also, because this was a first for Copy and no one knows how a two year old colt is going to act, I did not want Jamie to ride him. I told Virginia and Jamie that I would give it a try. I let the stirrups out on the racing saddle as far as they would go – which was not very far. I got a boost up on Copy's back and when I put my feet in the stirrups, my knees were chin high.

Jamie had been holding Copy's reins but now let go so I could warm him up a little. Needless to say, Copy was in very good condition and having waited around for a couple of hours was, as they say, on his toes. He began prancing around and lunging against the bit, and I kept falling forward on to his neck and falling back on his rear end. I thought, "This is ridiculous, when he breaks out of the gate, if I get that far, I'll probably fall off. What will that do to his preparation for the official schooling race?"

I don't know how, but I managed to stay on him through the warm up process. Jamie had already entered the gates on Lusty when we loaded Copy. He was relatively calm and quiet in the gates. I gathered up the reins and took a hold of as much mane as I could grab. I was scared to death and I'm sure it showed in more ways than just my shaking. Jamie who was in the stall next to me looked over and said, "Don't be scared, Dad". This did little to comfort me. How could this little 90 lb. girl think she should tell me not to be scared?

At any rate, the time had come. I told my friend to pull the rope to open the gates. Though the gates took only a fraction of a second to open, it seemed like an eternity. As they opened, Copy was ready to go. In three full strides, with me desperately clinging to his mane, he was going full speed. It turned out to be one of the smoothest rides I had ever experienced. A horse's run is the easiest of all its gaits. As we were heading down the track, I was really relieved, but also pretty proud. As I went past the grandstands, I could see that Virginia was facing away from the track.

When I put the brakes on to slow Copy down, he started prancing and lunging again. I fell against his neck and at this point I didn't care to stay on any longer, I just grabbed him around the neck and rolled off – exhilarated and relieved.

Now I have had some pretty fast cars in my life, but none of them could go 0 to 40 in 1.2 seconds. I am glad that Copy could, and I'm glad that I had the privilege to experience that unique thrill. Nevertheless, I haven't ridden a racing saddle since.

Go Top Copy, winning at Raton, NM

Myka, Me & The Bull;
Axioms Galore

THERE IS AN OLD AXIOM – everyone knows what an axiom is, don't they? It is a self evident or universally recognized truth. The axiom I am thinking about is "the best way to work cattle quickly is slowly". This had been preached to me since I was a youngster working at my Aunt's sale barn in Texarkana. Even though I understand the axiom, and believe in it, sometimes circumstances dictate doing otherwise.

I was really desperate to get one of my herd bulls penned, loaded and shipped before 4:00 pm one afternoon. I had a must attend meeting that evening. When I balanced getting the bull shipped and going to the meeting, they were pretty much even. But, since getting the bull in came first in the day and things got somewhat out of hand, I sort of forgot about the "working cattle slowly" axiom.

Another axiom, not as universally held but as true, is "don't bring one, bring 'em all". When you want to bring in one critter from the pasture the best way to do it is bring in the whole bunch and then sort out the one you wanted in the first place.

Well, the bull I wanted was with about 25 cows in a very rough 500 acre pasture. I was leasing the pasture from my daughter Myka's mother-in-law. The pasture was beautiful and productive but trying to round up cattle in it was a challenge. Since Myka knew the pasture and was a good hand, I elicited her help rounding up the cattle. We started early but by the time we got all of the cows together, along with the bull, it was getting late and approaching my deadline. That's when I sort of abandoned the first axiom.

Myka and I were both riding "bullet proof" horses. I was riding a black gelding named "Whiskey" that you could do anything on. If you were sorting cattle, he somehow knew exactly what you wanted to do. He was always in the right spot to get the job done. You could rope off him and know that he would not jerk down. He was one of those special horses that if you were on him and found yourself in trouble, it was probably your fault, not his.

After getting the cows gathered we pushed them as fast as we could into the main corral. This did not present a major problem, except that we now had 25 tired cows and one agitated bull. This is where things started to get rough. Once in the corral we had to push them into a smaller pen leading to the loading chute. The gate going into the chute pens was not very big and was in the center of the fence with no wing to head the cattle through the gate, which brings up the third axiom, "get prepared ahead of time". We should have put up two or three panels to create a wing.

We made three or four attempts to put the cattle in the chute pens with no success. We would get a few cows to go in but the bull, which was the center of our attention, would head off to one side. When we went to get him and bring him back, the cows we had in the pen would come back out.

Rather than stop and let the cows settle down and put some panels up, I looked at my watch and decided that I had to do something in a hurry. I told Myka to get the cattle prod out of the back of the truck. I had decided that I was going to rope the bull and pull him in the direction of the gate and she could get behind him using the prod and her horse to help move him forward. I got the rope on the bull and took about ten dallies.

This idea seemed to work pretty well until we got about twenty feet from the gate. The bull was no longer just agitated, he was mad. He balked and no matter how hard Whiskey pulled from the front and how hard Myka beat on his rear end, we couldn't move him. I thought I might be able to get his attention if I let a little slack in the rope and made a run toward the gate hoping to jerk him along. When I hit the end of my rope it spun Whiskey around so that we were broadside in front of the bull. That's when he decided he would move. He made a charge at Whiskey's mid section. The good pony that he was, Whiskey deftly moved forward to dodge the bull and let him pass behind us. The problem with this maneuver was that the rope got under Whiskey's tail and as the bull hit the end of the rope all hell broke loose. Not only was the rope under Whiskey's tail, it also had my leg pinned to the saddle.

Whiskey went to bucking and I desperately tried to unwrap the series of dallies I had taken. This took about 30 seconds which seemed like an hour. As soon as my leg was unpinned I bucked off hitting my head on the corral fence. I was lying on my back in the corral, bleeding from my head when Myka and her mother-in-law, who had been watching from the fence, came running over to me. The first thing Myka's mother-in-law said was that she was going to call 911. I told her that I thought I was okay and she had better not call anyone, I still had a meeting to go to.

Myka was very complementary. She said, "Dad, that was a great ride, Whiskey was really bucking hard and you rode him for a good 30 seconds". I told her, "Honey, there is no way I could get bucked off, I was tied on". After twenty years, I still have a crease on my leg where the rope had pinned me to the saddle.

As I lay there dazed and bleeding the fourth axiom came to me, "When you go to rope a bull, don't tie him to your tree."

The Great American Trailer Race

ONE OF THE FEW THINGS I did, that I probably would not have done had I given it much thought, was run for a spot on the Elbert County Fair Board. Unfortunately I was elected. It was a rather thankless job that took up way too much time. One of the many responsibilities of the fair board was producing a rodeo every year. I'm not sure how or why, but one day I found myself in charge of putting it on. I assume I was appointed to the position at one of the board meetings I failed to attend.

The Rodeo usually lasted two very long days because of the many events and the large number of contestants. Even though the fair board added some money to the purses, the bulk of the prize money came from the entry fees paid by the participants. Because of the number of contestants in each event the purses were pretty big. This was a time when ranchers and ranch hands came together not only to show off their horses and their skills but, if lucky, put a little jingle in their jeans. The competition was good natured but fierce.

There was one family, the Blasingames, that always came prepared to win every event. They were the sons and daughters of a ranching family that did everything on horseback as opposed to using a truck or 4-wheelers. In the winter they fed their cattle using horse drawn wagons instead of tractors. Their Mother delivered the mail on horseback. This family was not wealthy. Like most of us, they were struggling to get along. They believed in hard work and having good horses that were well trained and prepared for the task at hand. They were well liked and respected by everyone. Every year they expected, and usually did earn a little extra cash at the rodeo.

This particular year they entered most of the events, but by their standards, were not winning as much as they had in mind. The last event and the one which had the biggest purse and the most entertainment value was the trailer race. The rules for the race were long and specific. Bear with me as we go through them because they are important in evaluating the performance of Tom and Jim Blasingame.

Rules for the two man teams:

1. A horse trailer with one horse in it is backed into one end of the arena to a designated line. The horse had to be facing the front of the trailer and have a halter with a lead rope on it.

2. A saddle and bridle had to be in the bed of the pick-up which was attached to the horse trailer. The reins of the bridle and all attachments to the saddle had to

be fully contained in the bed of the pickup. Nothing could be hanging out.

3. The two contestants that made up the team had to be in the cab of the pickup with the doors shut.

4. When the flagger signaled to start the clock, the contestants had to get out of the truck, get the saddle and bridle and unload the horse.

5. They had to replace the halter with the bridle and saddle the horse.

6. One contestant had to ride the horse around a barrel at the far end of the area and return to the trailer.

7. They had to unsaddle the horse, replace the bridle with the halter, load the horse in the trailer and close and secure the trailer doors.

8. The time stopped when the saddle and bridle were put back in the bed of the pickup, with nothing hanging out, and both contestants were back in the pickup with the doors shut.

Looking at these rules it is easy to see what all can and usually does go wrong. Start with getting the horse unloaded. Generally speaking a horse is not going to back out of a trailer without some encouragement. You have to at least tug on the lead rope to let him know it's time to get out. The more excited the person is, trying to get him out; the less likely he is going to want to come out. Then, when you finally do get him out and the contestant is frantically grabbing at his head to get the halter off, he is further confused and wants to back up, all of this, while the other contestant is trying to throw a saddle on his back. It makes for quite a show. When you do get the saddle on you have to tighten the cinch and secure it to keep it from slipping off when you get on and during the ride around the barrel. Finally, how do you load a horse back into the trailer after the abuse he's just been through? It's not likely that he is going to just calmly step into the trailer.

As you can imagine, with horses running loose, cowboys getting run over, saddles slipping under the horses' bellies and riders getting bucked off, it was a crowd pleasing event. That is why the grandstands were always full for this event.

After about 20 teams had competed, with less than half completing the race, the best time was three minutes flat. Then came Tom and Jim with their last chance to make this a successful day, and they gave a spectacular performance.

Tom was in the driver's seat and Jim was on the passenger side. Trixie, one of their best trained mares, was in the trailer. When the flag dropped Tom jumped out, grabbed the saddle and bridle from the back of the truck, and Jim hurried to the rear of the trailer to open the door. Trixie, being well trained, without any encouragement, backed out of the trailer in a rush. As she backed out, Jim grabbed the halter, pulling it off, and wrapped his arm around her neck to allow Tom, who dropped the saddle at Trixie's side, to slip the bridle on. While Tom was putting the bridle on, Jim picked up the saddle and put it on Trixie's back. Rather than take the time to buckle the cinch, he pulled it tight and took two dallies around the saddle horn. Jim grabbed the reins from Tom and headed Trixie toward the barrel. In typical pony express fashion he jumped on her while she was going full speed and made the trip around the barrel and back toward the trailer. About half way back, he unwrapped his dallies and jumped off the mare taking the saddle with him. Tom grabbed the bridle reins, took the bridle off and on the run slipped the halter on. Trixie, almost at a full run, jumped in the trailer and the door was closed behind her. Jim threw the saddle in the back of the pickup and Tom threw the bridle in. Both jumped in the pickup and slammed the doors shut, all in 58 seconds.

However, as the flag dropped, the flagger noticed that one of the bridle reins was hanging out of the rear of the pickup gate by about two inches. This was announced to the crowd over the loud speaker. The announcer said that Tom and Jim were disqualified. The crowd shouted their disapproval and became downright unruly. I was called in to review the situation and see if I could calm things down. I made an executive decision. Rather than automatically disqualifying them, I assessed a two minute penalty. After reviewing all the other times, Tom and Jim were declared the winner by two seconds. The second place finishers, being the good sports they were, actually supported my decision, as did the crowd. Everybody recognized that they had witnessed an outstanding display of horsemanship.

The Illegal Immigrant,
a Valued Employee

ONE VERY COLD AND RAINY March morning in Colorado, Virginia had to drive the 75 miles into Denver for a meeting. Nothing was too unusual about this, but I did worry about her with the weather conditions being what they were. Everything went OK and she got back safe about 4:00 in the afternoon.

We had been invited to dinner that evening by our neighbors (closest neighbors) who lived about three miles down the highway toward Denver. We were supposed to be there at 6:30 so we got all gussied up to drive to our neighbor's house. By this time however, the rain, mixed with snow, had turned into a pretty good spring snow storm. It was dark and the visibility was not good.

Because of the snowy conditions we were driving pretty slow and we noticed a man walking toward us along the road. As we passed him Virginia said, "I think that is the same person I saw walking along the highway this morning". I asked her where she had seen him and she said that it was near the town of Elizabeth, which was about thirty miles from our ranch. We decided that we had better check into the situation. I turned the truck around and pulled up beside him. Virginia rolled down her window to talk to him and at first there was a lot of apprehension on his face. Virginia asked him if he needed any help and because of her tone of voice the apprehension disappeared. In the next couple of seconds it was evident that we had a serious communication problem. He didn't speak English and neither Virginia nor I spoke much Spanish. We did however ascertain that he was very cold, wet and hungry. We had a little efficiency apartment in our barn and we decided to take him back to the ranch and let him stay in the apartment for the night. When we got back to the headquarters, Virginia ran into the house to fix him a sandwich and I showed him to the apartment. We explained to him as best we could that we would be back in a couple of hours.

While we were having dinner, we told our neighbors what had happened and that we were a little bit concerned about having left this person at the barn. After all, the barn was only a hundred yards or so from the house and all of the doors and windows were unlocked. We had lived there about ten years and had never had the occasion to lock our doors. Even though we were a little apprehensive, we did think everything was going to be okay. Even with the communication gap, our first impression was that this was a fairly decent guy.

We asked our neighbors for some of the leftovers from

dinner to take to our guest, which they very obligingly provided. When we got back to the ranch I went to the barn and found our guest warm and content in the bed. I gave him the excellent dinner leftovers and he was very appreciative.

I went to the house and was feeling very pleased and Good Samaritan like.

The next morning, before dawn, I ventured down to the barn to check on our overnight guest. I found him already fully dressed and impatient to be doing something. He could understand English better than I could speak Spanish, and I was able to convince him to come to the house for some coffee and breakfast. When he came to the house, he brought with him, the duffle bag he was carrying when we picked him up.

While we were eating breakfast, we learned that his name was Juan José Mares. As he finished eating, he dug into his pocket and pulled out a beautiful pearl handled pocket knife. He tried to give it to me in appreciation for what we had done. I refused it and tried to explain that it was not necessary. I think he misunderstood me and thought I did not like the knife, because he went to his duffle bag and pulled out a nice clean denim shirt and offered it to me. I again refused his gift and he, as he had before, looked concerned that I did not like what he was trying to give me.

As you might expect there had not been much conversation during breakfast but, after breakfast he tried to tell us that he would like to do some work. At first, I thought he was asking for a job but he finally got across to us that he wanted to do some work to pay for his room and board. I really couldn't come up with anything for him to do on the spur of the moment, but knew that it was important to him that I find something.

The sun had come up and even though cold, about 20 degrees, it was going to be a beautiful day. We went outside and I asked myself what do I usually do first thing in the morning. The answer was that I would break the ice on the nearby water tanks and fill them up. There were three tanks within a quarter of a mile of the house where we watered our horses and the cattle that we were keeping close in. Each of the tanks was on a pipeline and had a frost free hydrant used to fill them. I picked up an axe to break the ice and we walked to the nearest tank. Again, as best I could, I told him to break the ice and take the bigger chunks of ice out of the tank and then fill it up. I pointed out the other two tanks and told him to do the same with them. I went back to the house to discuss with Virginia what we were going to do with Sr. Mares.

About an hour and a half went by and we had not seen anything of our new worker. At first I thought that he had solved our problem of what we were going to do with him, and he had just gone on his way. Then I noticed the duffle bag on the kitchen floor and figured that he wouldn't leave that behind, so I went to check on what had happened to him.

I found him still at the first of the three tanks. He had cleaned every chunk of ice out of the tank and was messing with the hydrant. He was pumping the handle like you would a pump that you used to see on a well or at a kitchen sink. It had never occurred to me that he had never seen a frost free hydrant. Every time he pulled the hydrant handle up a little spurt of water would come out, but when he pushed it back down the water flow would stop. At this rate it would take a considerable amount of time to fill the 250 gallon tank. I had a little chuckle and showed him that if you just pulled the handle up and didn't push it back down, the water would flow continuously. When he saw that, we both had a good chuckle. I told him to go do the other tanks and that I would shut the water off when this tank was full and for him to come to the house when he got through.

He was back at the house in about 30 minutes and we were ready to face our next challenge. Virginia had gotten her Spanish-English dictionary out and we were determined to find out why Juan had been walking along the road on such a cold and miserable night, and where he was going.

Because of our earlier attempts at communicating with Juan, Virginia and I knew that our next challenge would be daunting. From the time we had picked him up we had probably effectively communicated twenty words between us and most of them were because of his understanding of English as opposed to our understanding of Spanish. But, equipped with the Spanish-English dictionary, we were bound and determined to find the answers to our questions.

After about an hour of intense stressful work we finally determined (at that point we at least thought we did) that he worked for a big ranch around Ozona, Texas. He had worked there several years, and every winter he would go back to Mexico for a couple of months to visit his family. On this particular occasion he had hitched a ride back to Texas on a truck with a bunch of other immigrants that were being taken to Greeley, Colorado to work in the beet fields. The driver of the truck was supposed to drop him off in Texas in the vicinity of Ozona but failed to do so. Juan woke up one morning in northern Colorado. He didn't have any money so his only alternative was to start walking back to Texas. Virginia and I had picked him up on the second day of his trek. The night before, he had slept in a culvert under the road.

We then set about trying to find out the name of the ranch and the names of the people he worked for. We finally determined that the owner of the ranch was named Herman Williams. We called information in Ozona and there was no listing for either a Herman Williams or a Williams' ranch. We checked our Texas map and got the names of a couple of small towns near Ozona. We finally found a listing for an H. A. Williams Ranch and called the number not knowing what to expect. A woman answered the phone and I asked if this was the Williams residence and she answered, "Yes, this is Mrs. Williams." I then explained to her who I was, where I lived and the purpose of my call. When I told her that we had a visitor named Juan José Mares, who claims to work for her ranch, she said "Oh my gosh, I'll let you talk to my husband".

Shortly, what sounded like an elderly gentleman came to the phone and I went over with him the various happenings of the last couple of days. He was ecstatic and said that Juan was one of his best hands. He added that he had expected him back two weeks ago, and he really did need him, as they were supposed to start branding in a couple of days.

Having established that Juan had a home, the next task was how do we get him the 800 miles from where he was to where he was supposed to be. Mr. Williams asked if there was a bus line near where I lived. I told him that we were about 40 miles from Limon, Colorado, which was located on U.S. Highway 287. I didn't know for sure, but I thought they would have bus service. Since 287 went through Amarillo, I felt certain we could get him that far at least. Herman (we were on a first name basis by now) asked me to check the bus schedule and see if we put Juan on a bus in Limon could he eventually end up in Ozona. I looked up a number for Continental Bus Lines and found that there was a bus that went through Limon and went directly to Amarillo, but there he would have to transfer to Greyhound to get to Ozona. This sounded simple enough, so I called Herman back and explained that Juan would have to transfer from Continental to Greyhound in Amarillo. Herman said that he would reimburse me for my expenses and pay me for my time if I would put Juan on the bus as soon as possible. He added that he was concerned because immigration agents were known for picking up illegals in the Amarillo area. With this in mind, Virginia set out to explain to Juan that it was important that he get from the Continental bus terminal to the Greyhound bus terminal as quickly and quietly as possible. We didn't know where either bus station was located, but hoped they were located in the same terminal.

We weren't so lucky. After calling both Continental and Greyhound, we found out that Continental was located on Taylor Street in Amarillo and that Greyhound was located about three blocks away on Tyler Street. Virginia and I looked at each other and said how do we possibly explain to Juan that in order to change buses, he needed to get from the Continental Depot on Taylor Street to the Greyhound Depot on Tyler Street. Even using the Spanish- English dictionary this seemed to be an impossible task.

After another hour or so of intense effort, which included drawing a map and spelling out Taylor and Tyler, we were not sure that Juan understood what we were trying to tell him. Our time was running out because we had to get him to Limon to catch the bus at 3:00 p.m. In desperation, we decided to call Herman. When Herman got on the phone, I asked him if he spoke Spanish, which, of course, he did. I explained our dilemma and asked him to speak to Juan to see if he understood what he had to do. I told Herman that he had only 45 minutes to change buses. I put Juan on the phone and after a couple of minutes he handed the phone back to me. Herman said that we had done a great job because Juan knew exactly what he had to do. Virginia and I were both pretty proud, and Virginia even considered applying for a position at the local high school teaching Spanish.

Virginia packed Juan a lunch and I gave him a $20.00 bill. We took him to Limon to catch the bus and waited around until he got on. Just before boarding, he hugged both of us and in very clear English, said "Thank you very much for all you did".

When we got home, I called Herman and told him that Juan was on his way. He asked me what I owed him and I told him that the ticket amounted to $77.50. He said he would put a check in the mail that day.

The next night, Herman called and said that Juan had made it. He was very grateful. A couple of days later I got a check drawn on the First National Bank of Ozona for $177.50. That was more money than I made on my cattle that year. Two days later, I got another check drawn on the same bank for $20.00.

This was my first up close and personal experience with an illegal immigrant and I was pleasantly surprised. Juan was a hardworking, appreciative gentleman who earned my respect as he had won the respect of Mr. Williams. Later contacts with illegals confirmed my first impression. For some reason, this was a very important event in my life.

Champagne Lady II
and the Pony Express Race

IN A LOT OF MY stories I have written about the many truly magnificent horses I have had the privilege to own. One of the best was a mare by the name of Champagne Lady II. Her name was indicative of her breeding. She was the daughter of Jet Deck, who during his racing career was named 1962 Champion Stallion, 1963 Champion Stallion and 1963 World Champion by the American Quarter Horse Association. His greatest contribution to the breed, however, was as a sire. In only eight foal crops he sired 5 AQHA Champions, 1 Supreme Champion and 383 Race Registers of Merit.

From the day we bought her and brought her home we called her "Bubbles". It was a very appropriate name. Not only did her registered name, Champagne Lady II, and her impeccable breeding inspire the nickname Bubbles, but that was also her personality. She was truly a vivacious dame.

When we bought Bubbles she was a three year old filly that was preg checked in foal to another prestigious Quarter

Horse sire, "Three Ohs". She came with a live foal guarantee, which meant that if she did not have a live foal, we had the right to breed her back to Three Ohs, free of charge. The farm that bred her, and we bought her from, had chosen not to run her because she had one slightly crooked leg that might have caused her to break down.

Bubbles was due to foal in late January, but sometime around the middle of December she slipped her foal. This, of course, was very disheartening. We were looking forward to having one of the best bred foals in the country. We had Woody, our vet, check her to see if there was a problem that might carry over. He didn't find anything so on the first day of February we took her back to Three Ohs.

We kept close tabs on her at the breeding farm and in late March she was again preg checked in foal. We brought her home and this time we kept her in a small pasture near the barn with one other gentle mare. We carefully measured her progress, but again she aborted. We had Woody check her again and he discovered a possible problem with the lining of her uterus. We took her to the CSU Veterinary School of Medicine, recognized as one of the best in the country, and Woody's diagnosis was confirmed. After a couple thousand dollars of testing and treatment, CSU determined that it was unlikely that she would be able to carry a foal to term.

So what do you do with a very expensive, lovable, five year old brood mare that can't have a foal? We decided to break her and use her as a ranch horse. Because of her intelligence and her willingness to work, Bubbles was very easy to break. When we started using her, we discovered that like most quarter horses, she had a natural ability to work cattle. She anticipated their every move and was so quick that hardly anything got by her. We also realized that true to her breeding, she was very fast. She could cover ground unlike any horse I had ever ridden.

In the spring of Bubbles' seven year old year, a group of horsemen from several neighboring counties organized a pony express race. They raised quite a bit of money for the purse and advertised it to attract the best horses in the area. The race was to be two miles long with one change of horses at the half way mark.

This sounded like a good opportunity to recoup some of the money I had in Bubbles. Not only did I have her, I also had Lusty, who was an old hand at this sort of thing, and both of them were in excellent condition. Now, all I needed was a good rider that could change and mount a running horse "pony express" style. Darrell, one of Woody's assistant vets, told me that he had ridden in some pony express type races in Canada and that he would like to ride the race. I asked him to come out to the ranch and we would see how Bubbles and Lusty would react to the running remount procedure. After a couple of practice sessions things were looking good. Darrell was an expert at making the change. We decided that Lusty should start the race because we knew that there would be a lot of confusion at the start and as I said earlier, this was not new to him. It was three weeks until the race, and Jamie worked both Bubbles and Lusty for a mile or better several times to get them used to the distance.

For the race, a two mile track was staked out on the side of a gently sloping hill so that the race could be viewed in its entirety by people gathered at the starting point. It was a perfect cross country setting and the crowd was big and enthusiastic. Jamie was assigned the duty of holding Bubbles and positioning her for a quick running mount by Darrell. Jamie knew both Bubbles and Lusty very well and I knew that if anybody could keep Bubbles calm, she could.

There were nine teams in the race. I thought we had a chance but there were some very good horses that I knew, and some that I did not know anything about. The race started as I thought it would. Lusty was quiet but ever ready to go. He jumped out in front but only by the narrowest of margins. However, by the half mile pole he was a good ten lengths ahead. I was feeling pretty confident because with Bubbles' speed and conditioning, we should easily win the race.

By the time Lusty reached the exchange point he was at least 14 or 15 lengths in front. Darrell slid him to a stop and jumped off. Jamie led Bubbles at a run in front of him and Darrell jumped on her with ease. Everything seemed to be going well when all of a sudden Darrell abruptly stopped Bubbles and reversed direction. I didn't know what the hell was going on but I didn't like it. Then I saw that Jamie had picked something up off the ground and was running toward Bubbles and Darrell. Jamie had picked up the "mail bag" that

Darrell had dropped and which had to be carried across the finish line. Darrell grabbed the bag from Jamie and rejoined the race.

By this time all but two of the teams had passed us. When Bubbles turned to get back in the race she exploded. She began closing the gap between her and those in front of her with every stride. With a little more than a quarter mile to go she had passed all but two of the horses and was still gaining. We had a chance but it was going to be close. When the crowd realized what had happened, and saw the tremendous effort by Bubbles, they were rooting for her, even those that had horses in the race. In the last quarter mile Bubbles caught the leading team and won by a half length. You can't believe how I felt.

As Darrell brought her back to the starting point I ran and hugged her. I told her "I'm sort of glad you couldn't have a foal," and I said to Darrell, "You better be glad Bubbles saved your hide."

We had several years of good happenings with Bubbles. Myka and Jamie used her in various gymkhana events, we won races with her on the bush tracks, and more than anything, we constantly relied on her to help out on the ranch. I feel very fortunate to have had her.

Night Work and Barbed Wire Fences

My son-in-law, Pat, and I were running some first calf heifers in Colorado one year. We had bred them to a good low birth weight Angus bull for calving ease, but knew that we would have to keep close tabs on them, and probably have to pull a couple of calves.

We had leased a small pasture that had not been grazed for a couple of years and was lush with buffalo grass. It was pretty open country but had a good stand of ponderosa pine and scrub oak that would provide excellent protection during a winter storm. The fences were adequate but not very tight. The one big problem was that it was about 30 miles from our ranch headquarters. Normally you want your first calf heifers close by so that you can check them often, even a couple of times during the night. Also, because of the distance it was not practical to ride through them on horseback. We had to drive around in a pickup to get close enough to make sure everything was okay. This was difficult to do because, even in the open areas, the pasture was rough and had a series of draws that made it difficult to negotiate in a vehicle.

The heifers were due to start calving around the first of February, so beginning on the 20th of January we started checking them twice a day. By the tenth of February, we had twelve calves on the ground and had not had a problem. The calves were relatively small and the heifers had calved easily. We were feeling pretty good about our heifer and bull selections and relaxed our checking procedures a bit. Rather than two times a day, we went to once a day. Because heifers generally calve during the night we would try to check them early in the morning just after daylight, but this was not always possible or practical.

One Sunday morning neither Pat nor I were able to check the heifers, so that afternoon I went to the pasture to see how things were going. As I drove through the gate going into the pasture I saw that we had two new, healthy calves. I drove through the herd and did not see any indication that there was a problem. Then, I saw a heifer standing a considerable distance away from the others, which usually meant that she was at least thinking about calving. She was on the other side of a steep gully that would have been difficult to cross in the truck, so I drove to the edge of the gully to get close enough to see if I could determine if anything was wrong. After a few minutes she laid down and I thought everything was going to be okay. I watched her for about an hour and now I was getting concerned. At the distance I was from her I really couldn't tell exactly what was going on, so I decided to cross the gully on foot to get close enough to see what was happening. When I approached her I could see that one of the calf's front legs was out. I stayed at a distance for awhile, thinking that she might be able to push the calf the rest of the way out. When it looked like this was not going to happen, I reluctantly decided to approach her to see if I could help. I knew that sometimes when a cow is having trouble calving you can approach her and she won't try to get up. You can then help by pulling the calf. However, this was not the case this time. I got a few feet from her and she jumped up and headed for the stand of trees. I knew that I was going to need help if I was going to be of any help to her, so I ran back to the truck and went to find Pat. He was at his house, and we rushed back to the pasture.

By this time, it was getting pretty dark. We circled around the deep gully and were able to drive to the trees where we thought she would be. With the help of a flashlight, we found her lying down. We walked very slowly toward her, again hoping that she would stay down. I had a lariat and was prepared to rope her if necessary. When we got to within about 10 feet of her, she jumped up. I was able to get a rope on her as she started to run away. Now the question was whether I could hold on when she hit the end of the rope. I knew we were close to a corner of the pasture and that there was a fence to my left and to Pat's right, but because of the darkness I didn't know how close we were. The heifer, because she could see a lot better in the dark, knew that she was in a corner and she attempted to run past me on my left. I ran as hard as I could to head her off, hoping to keep her in the corner until we could snub her to one of the trees. As I broke to my left she went around a tree, and the rope wrapped around the tree which helped to slow her down. With the rope around the tree and me yelling, she turned back. I was still running to make sure she didn't get out of the corner when I hit the fence. It was not very tight and it sort of just laid over with me on top of it. I was parallel to the ground about two feet in the air. I couldn't reach the ground with either my feet or my hands. I was helpless and I could feel all four strands of barbed wire digging into me from my knees to my chest. I said to myself, "How the hell am I going to get off this fence?" Every time I tried to move the barbs sank in deeper.

Looking over my shoulder I could see that Pat had snubbed the heifer to the tree that she had wrapped herself around. I was still contemplating my predicament when I saw him walking toward me grinning from ear to ear. He said, "Come on, we have to pull this calf." Obviously, he didn't know how much I was hurting and I was afraid he was going to grab my boots and try to pull me off the fence. I knew this would only make matters worse and I said "Pat, you son of a bitch, don't you touch me." His grin turned into a laugh as he walked over to get a closer look. He was strong as an ox, and when he realized how I was trapped on the fence, he reached down and grabbed me by my belt and lifted me straight up. I think it was the only possible way to get me off of the fence without causing a lot more pain. I was grateful for what he did, but I didn't say anything, I was still mad at him for laughing at the predicament I had been in.

When I realized I wasn't going to bleed to death, we snubbed the heifer up tight and pulled the calf, which was alive and well. We named him "Barbed Wire".

Mesa Redonda

Bandit, supervising Boss milking wild cow

Jamie and Author on Mesa Redonda

Family Picture

Myka on Otis, cutting competition

Big Boy at El Cross Ranch in East Texas

Speckles at El Cross Ranch in East Texas

Author and Grandson , PJ

Virginia and Grandson, Brian

PJ on Amigo

Brian on Flight Bit

View from the top

Another view of Canyon pasture

Politics in the Work Place

IN MY PREVIOUS STORIES I have tried to stay on subject (ranching experiences I have had) and have not talked politics. Those of you who know me, know how hard this must be. However, with the recent change to Daylight Savings Time, I feel like I have to speak out. Why would any politician, especially those that espouse "less government" think they should interfere in a person's life to the extent of determining when they should get up and when they should go to bed?

It just doesn't make sense. This is especially true to those of us who have animals to care for. Can you imagine trying to explain the change in feeding time to 300 mother cows? One Spring day you are feeding them at 5:30 am and the next day at 4:30 am. I have had this conversation with my cows, but they just don't get it. They can't understand why if you take one hour off of daylight in the morning and add it to the daylight in the evening you have somehow saved daylight.

Moving on, I also have a similar disdain for the seat

belt laws. But, as with the time change, I was reluctant to speak out until an event occurred one Sunday morning in New Mexico. Shortly after moving to the "land of enchantment" my wife and I were driving some friends that had spent the night with us the twelve miles into Tucumcari for breakfast. I was not in a hurry, so I wasn't speeding. We were just visiting and enjoying the scenery when we met an oncoming state patrolman. As we passed him, he turned on his overheads and through my rear view mirror, I saw him turn around. Since I was the only other vehicle on the twelve mile stretch of road between the ranch and town, I surmised that he was after me. I pulled over, and again through my rear view mirror, I saw the officer get out of his patrol car, ticket book in hand, and swagger up to my window. I said to him, "Officer, this may be a first, but I wasn't speeding or doing anything wrong." He said you weren't wearing your seat belt and we have a dim view of outsiders (I still had Colorado tags on my truck) driving on our streets and highways without wearing a seat belt. After taking my Colorado drivers license and proof of insurance, he went back to his vehicle. Twenty minutes later he came back and handed me a ticket. This was not a very good start to my Sunday morning and it made a lasting impression on me.

I followed the instructions on the ticket and mailed in the fine. However, this experience kept eating away at me so I figured I had to speak out. I sent the following letter to the New Mexico Department of Public Safety.

POLITICS IN THE WORK PLACE

Department of Public Safety

Dear Sir:

A couple of months ago I began having severe pains is my left arm and shoulder. After a couple of weeks the pain was so great I decided to see my Doctor in Tucumcari. After a series of tests and x-rays, my local Doctor was befuddled and he referred me to a sports medicine specialist in Albuquerque. The specialist very quickly diagnosed my condition as "seat belt elbow", an injury caused by quickly reaching for your seat belt every time you see a cop.

The Doctor prescribed painkillers and cortisone shots. After two of the shots and receiving the bill from the Doctor, I quickly determined that I could not afford to continue with this kind of treatment. As an alternative, the Doctor recommended that rather than reaching for my seat belt when I saw a policeman and then releasing it when he passed, that I simply pull the seat belt down and hold it in my lap.

This seemed like a sensible solution to my problem, that is until I was driving down the highway that goes past my ranch and a state patrol car came toward me from the opposite direction,. As is the custom in many rural areas, I raised my hand to waive at the officer as he passed, Not only did he see that I wasn't wearing my seat belt, he actually thought I was thumbing my nose at him.

The resulting ticket cost me more than twice the cost of the cortisone shots.

It is apparent that the seat belt law as presently written and the diligent efforts to enforce it by the local patrolmen is the cause of my medical condition. I would appreciate it if you would inform your Tucumcari office that they should ease up in enforcing this law and go after the real criminals.

Please let me know when this new policy will go into effect.

I am sure you can see the reasonableness of my request. If for some reason you do not agree with me and continue with the vigorous enforcement policy now in effect, I may be forced to take legal action. If I do, I will ask the Court to issue an injunction prohibiting the enforcement of the law and I will also seek damages to cover my medical costs and my pain and suffering. The sports injury doctor has advised me that he is seeing more and more patients with this ailment and, as a result, any lawsuit filed by me may blossom into a full-fledged class action.

I want to thank you for your attention to this matter and look forward to hearing from you soon.

Concerned Citizen

P.S. I hope that when we get this issue straightened out we can discuss the DUI laws.

P.S. #2 On a personal note, I would like to make a special request. I get up every morning about 5:00 a.m., but by the time I get through with chores and get to town for breakfast, all of the doughnuts are gone. Please ask your patrolmen to leave me a couple of raspberry filled donuts every morning.

Although I did not receive a response from the Department of Public Safety, there were always a couple of raspberry filled doughnuts at the doughnut shop after that.

Tip of The Day

WHEN VIRGINIA AND I WERE looking at the ranch in New Mexico, we knew that we were going to have a snake problem. When we drove by the High School in Tucumcari we found out that the team mascot was a rattle snake and the banner over the gymnasium door read "Welcome to the Snake Pit". Also, when you stop at the beautiful rest stops along the interstate in that part of the country, the first thing you see when you get out of your vehicle is a warning sign, "Watch out for rattlesnakes", and, in exploring the ranch we had a few up close and personal encounters.

We knew this was somewhat of a problem but certainly not anything that could not be overcome. We learned how and when to be aware and careful. You keep in mind precautions that you need to take when you encounter a potentially dangerous situation.

There was, however, one situation that I had not anticipated or prepared for, which leads to my "tip of the day". I was looking for some stray cows on our mesa when my horse jumped out from under me. On the way down I realized what spooked him. I heard the distinct buzzing of a big snake, but because of my hearing problem, I didn't know where the snake was. I was lying on my back not knowing what to do to get out of harms' way. I figured that the best thing I could do was to start rolling over and over to get away from the snake, but in which direction? Then it came to me. I thought "you idiot, roll in the direction the horse went when he bucked you off."

Now keep this in mind if this ever happens to you.

Results of a few close encounters

Getting To Know Your Cattle

ONE THING I HAVE LEARNED about ranching over the past several years is that it pays to know your cattle. Our ranch in New Mexico was, to say the least, very rough country. Part of the ranch consisted of the famous Mesa Redonda. The only way to the top of the mesa was a very narrow, steep trail that could only be negotiated on horseback or, on some occasions, (weather permitting) in a 4WD truck. We grazed the cattle on the bottom of the mesa during the winter and on top of the mesa during the summer. The cattle were moved to the top in the middle of May and brought back down around the first of October.

Realizing how rough the country was and how difficult it would be to drive the cattle up the narrow trail to the top, I bought a good number of cows from the previous owner of the ranch. I was really proud that I had thought of this. Obviously, it would help to have some cows that had made the trip to the top before and knew the way.

The first time we drove the cattle to the top, I learned a couple of new things. I was worried about the drive and really did not know what to expect. I put together a crew of seven cowboys to help. All of them were top hands and had made the drive before, which boosted my confidence.

This was my first year at the New Mexico ranch and the crew I put together didn't know me very well. Whenever I would ask any of them for their advice in putting together a "plan", they were hesitant to give it. It was fairly obvious that they were afraid that if they gave me advice, it would imply that I did not know what I was doing, which I didn't.

On the day of the drive, we left the house at daybreak and rode to the holding pasture where we had the cows. We rounded them up and drove them to the gate leading to the trail up the mountain. This seemed to go well, as the cows, at least those I had bought from the previous owner, seemed to know the routine. One of the crew asked me if I wanted someone to ride ahead of the herd to sort of head them up. I asked him what he would do and true to form he said whatever I thought best. Since the cattle were moving so good I decided that it would not be necessary to have a lead rider.

Everything went well for the first three miles up the trail. Then, I learned the first lesson. The trail was so steep and difficult to traverse that the two and three month old calves were getting really tired, and began to fall back. It became harder and harder to push them to keep up with their mothers. As they strung out farther and farther behind the cows, the cows began to turn back to look for their calves. Now we had a situation where the calves did not want to go up and the cows were on their way back down. All we could do was let the cows find their calves and with a little bit of rest, start back up the hill. This problem could have been averted if I had had a lead rider in front of the cows to slow them down.

Everything went pretty well after that until the next little problem arose. About a mile from the top there was a false summit. The trail flattened out and somewhat opened up and there was nothing to keep the cattle on the straight and narrow. When they hit this area the cattle spread out on both sides, hiding in the thick cedars that lined the trail. One cowboy had to get off his horse to drive a brushed up cow and calf out into the open. He went through the cedars and successfully brought the pair out. But, when he turned around to get his horse the cedars were so thick he couldn't find it. The lesson learned was that we needed at least two riders ahead of the cows to prevent them from spreading out as they came to this more open area. Having had this experience on the first drive and being prepared on subsequent drives, most of them went about as well as could be expected.

Each time we brought the cattle down in the fall, things went well. After four or five summers it was pretty easy to predict how long it would take to either take them up or bring them down, at least until the summer of 2001. That was the first year of a severe drought that lasted five years. The cows were on top of the mesa and by the middle of August they were running low on water. I didn't want them to run completely out of water so I decided to bring them down early. I put together a crew and scheduled the day to bring them down.

A couple of weeks earlier, a friend of mine, Bill Curry, a famous western artist, had called and asked me to let him know when we were going to bring the cows off the mesa, because he wanted to come out and get some pictures of them coming down the steep trail. Bill had already painted several pictures of the Mesa and I was excited that he wanted to do this. I called him and told him the day we had scheduled to bring them down. He told me that he had somewhat of a problem with that day because he had a meeting that he had to attend at 3:30 p.m. on that afternoon. I, very confidently, told him that that would not be a problem because I knew that we would have all the cattle down the hill by 12:00 noon. Bill said that this would work and told me that he would be in place at the appropriate time.

As was the custom, on the day of the drive, all of the crew had breakfast at the house. We left the headquarters at day break and except for the fact that it was the middle of August, and very hot, instead of the first of October, everything was going as planned. We got the cattle rounded up and pushed them toward the trail going down. At the head of the trail, there was a huge open area with nothing to funnel the cattle onto the trail. This had never been a problem in the past as the cattle had always been eager to go down and lead the way.

I thought to myself that we were right on time and Bill

would be impressed that I had known exactly what time the cattle would be coming into his view. But, something happened that I had not expected. As the cattle approached the head of the trail they became increasingly nervous. Almost on cue they began to scatter and there was absolutely no way to hold them together. Had we anticipated that they were going to scatter we would have positioned ourselves a little better, but now all we could do was circle the herd in a wide arc to keep them from going to the opposite end of the mesa where we would have to start all over again.

We finally got them together and while they were settling down I realized what the problem was. The cows knew that it was not time to come off the mesa. They still had another month and a half on top. To overcome this clock in their head, we kept them pretty tightly bunched and moved them very slowly toward the top of the trail (the only way to move cattle in a hurry is s-l-o-w-l-y). We finally got a few of them started down the hill and as the other cows saw the few heading down they eventually followed. Of course, once on the trail because of how narrow it was we could push them down the rest of the way. As we past the point where Bill was going to take the pictures I looked at my watch and it was exactly 3:30. I was embarrassed, having been so confident of the time we would be at that point.

That evening when we finished up and I was unsaddling my horse, I was trying to figure out how I could explain all of this to Bill and apologize to him for wasting his time. When I went in the house there was a message on the answering machine. It was from Bill. He said, "Larry, I must have gotten the date wrong. I waited until 2:00 p.m. today and I didn't see any cows". I called Bill and left a message on his machine. I said "Yeah, Bill, I wondered what happened to you yesterday."

Cattle on trail coming off the mesa

Greatest Pitch I Ever Threw

IN HIGH SCHOOL I PLAYED second base on our baseball team. I was also the third pitcher in our starting rotation. I was not a very good pitcher but I did have excellent control. I could hit any spot over or around the plate. I just couldn't throw hard enough to do much with it.

In my junior year our team, the Catholic High Eagles of Texarkana, played for the State Championship against the Sacred Heart Tigers of Muenster, TX. The Championship was to be decided by a two out of three game series to be played over two weekends. This was good news to me because it meant that I would probably not have to pitch. The two starters ahead of me would have enough rest to pitch all three games if the series went that far.

Weather, however, became a major factor in the outcome of the series. The first game was to be played on a Saturday in Texarkana and the second and third games were to be played in Muenster the following weekend. The game in Texarkana was rained out and the "powers that be" decided that all three games would be played in Muenster on Saturday and Sunday of the following week. This meant that if the series went three games, I would have to pitch the third game. I secretly hoped that we would win or lose the series in two games. This was especially true when I saw the size of the Muenster boys and watched them take batting practice before the first game.

Muenster is a German town and the players were all big farm boys. One of them was a very big and very good fast ball pitcher, and because he often pitched batting practice, they had several good fast ball hitters. We had one of the best pitchers in Texas, by the name of Paul Schoen. He had a good fast ball but his forte was a curve ball that would break more than a foot and a half.

In the first inning of the first game, Paul struck out the first batter. The second batter connected with a fast ball to deep left center for a triple. After a brief discussion on the mound, everyone was in agreement that the fast ball was not going to be the pitch of the day. Paul struck out the next two batters, stranding the player on third. He then struck out the next 24 batters, all on curve balls.

Muenster's pitcher was almost as effective. In the seventh inning with the score tied at 0 – 0, one of our players connected with one of his fast balls for a solo home run. We went on to win the first game 1 – 0. We lost the second game 4 – 3 and the third game 11 – 2, but I want you to know I did not walk a batter.

Let's move on to the more spectacular event and the subject of this story. We were moving our cows to the top of our mesa in New Mexico. The trail was very steep and narrow. Close to the top there was a point where the trail was only about twenty-five feet wide. On one side there was a vertical wall that was about 30 feet high and on the other side there was a vertical drop off of about 25 feet, and then another 100 feet down to the canyon floor. Here, we had a gate that extended across the trail. This was to keep the cows on top of the mesa for the summer. There was no other way off.

From the gate, the top of the mesa was another half mile up the trail. No one could have anticipated what would happen as the cows approached the gate. Because of the narrow opening they bunched up and two of the cows were pushed off the trail down the steep embankment. Now, we had two cows that could not possibly climb back up to the trail and it would take days to go back and find a way through the canyon to where the cows may eventually end up. Without any hesitation my daughter, Jamie, a superb horsewoman, took her horse down the steep incline to try to keep the cows from going further down the canyon. As she approached the cows and tried to get in front of them the brush, cedars and terrain prevented her from doing so. The cows continued on their trek until they crossed a steep, narrow gully and were standing on the other side. Jamie was pretty much stymied at this point. She didn't want to go down into the gully, not knowing if she could climb back out to where the cows were, or what she could do if she were able to climb out. She yelled at the cows and waved her hat but the cows wouldn't move.

I yelled at her to see if she could work her way back up to the trail. As she was coming back up, I could see one of the cows. Her head was obscured by the brush and cedars, but I could see her from the neck back. She was probably 40 feet below me and 100 feet away. I had no idea what to do next but one thing I did know was that I was mad and it wouldn't bother me if I inflicted a little pain on those two cows.

I picked up a rock about 2 ½ inches in diameter and sort of tossed it in the direction of the visible cow. It came pretty close to her and I said to myself "maybe, I can hit the stupid b....." I found another rock of similar size, took careful aim and threw it as hard as I could in the direction of the cow. It was like I was in a zone. I knew I was going to hit her. Sure enough, I hit her right in the rib cage. She bawled and took off through the brush and cedars, and the other cow, which had been completely hidden, followed her. I did not know where they were going and at this point didn't much care. For a minute I thought back to the Muenster series and imagined that I had just struck out the last batter to win the third game. I was so in a trance that I turned around to tip my cap to the hundreds of adoring fans in the bleachers. Instead of cheering fans there were only a couple hundred cows and seven cowboys sitting on their horses staring at me, wondering what I was doing standing on the edge of the trail throwing rocks into the canyon.

We then started to push the cows on up the trail to the top. We rounded one bend in the trail and much to everyone's amazement, the two errant cows were standing on the trail in front of us. How they got out of that canyon is a complete mystery. All I know is that on that particular day I threw the perfect pitch.

Matt Martinez, Chef, Friend

As you may have gathered from previous stories, our ranch in New Mexico was rugged and beautiful, and owning it brought about many wonderful memories. I cherish all of those memories, but the friendships we developed while we were there are the most important. It would be impossible to list all of the friends we made and tell all of the stories connected with them but let me list a few. There was the Hight family, our closest neighbors; Don Hofman, the retired general manager of the Bell Ranch, one of the largest ranches in New Mexico; Frank "Frog" Robinson, a retired Navy man; and Don McKinley, whose day job was cowboying, and his night job was inventing. There are many others, the list is too long. Even though I have many stories to tell about all of these individuals, this is not the place to do it. However, before I get to Matt Martinez, the subject of this story, I do have to comment on my first meeting with Les Hight, the 80 year old patriarch of the Hight family.

I first met Les shortly after moving to the New Mexico ranch. We were sorting cattle at the headquarters when he stopped by. He introduced himself and asked me where I was from. I told him we had moved to New Mexico from eastern Colorado where we had ranched for several years. He then asked me what my neighbors were like in Colorado, and I told him they were absolutely great. He said you will like your neighbors here in New Mexico also. He then added, "Of course, if you had told me that you didn't like your Colorado neighbors, I would have told you that you were not going to like your neighbors here either." That exchange meant a lot to me and I knew this was going to be a good place to live.

One of the best friendships developed while living on the New Mexico ranch was between Matt and Estella Martinez and Virginia and me. Shortly after moving to New Mexico a lifelong friend of mine, Sonny Thomas, came to visit us at the ranch. He stayed a few days and after showing him around the ranch he said that he had a friend in Dallas named Matt Martinez who owned a couple of restaurants. One of the restaurants was "Rancho Martinez", and the other was called "No Place". Matt was an avid hunter and outdoorsman and he had formed a club that met every month or two at "No Place". On these occasions Matt would cook some exotic wild meat for the members and even though the dues were pretty pricey there was a long waiting list to get into the club. Sonny told me that Matt would love our ranch and probably would want to come out and hunt. I told Sonny to tell Matt that he would be welcome anytime.

A couple of weeks later we received an autographed copy of one of Matt's cookbooks, <u>Matt Martinez's Culinary Frontier</u>, with a handwritten personal note on the inside front cover.

Matt had also listed several phone numbers where he could be reached. After reading the great stories Matt had written for the book, Virginia and I thought this was a guy we would like to knows so we decided to give him a call. Virginia and I talked about it before I made the call and we both said, you know, if you call someone and say "why don't you come out sometime" it very seldom happens. So, we picked three dates and rather than just ask him to come out, I asked specifically if he could come out on a date certain. After a very long telephone conversation I was even more convinced that this was someone I really wanted to meet.

Polly Mullen © 2000

Matt and Pee Nutty on top of the mesa

A date was selected and sure enough Matt was coming. He drove out from Dallas in a Dodge Ram pickup accompanied by his rat terrier, "Pee Nutty" and one of his best friends, Grant Lappin, who was a Deputy Chief of Police for the City of Dallas. On the drive out Matt called several times. He wanted to know if we would like to have a few people over one evening, and if so, he would cook for them. We thought this sounded like a good idea so we put together a guest list and called him back. We asked if 16 people would be too many and he said that would be perfect. We then asked what we should get from the store for him to cook. He said not to worry; he had it all taken care of.

Well, when word got around that we were having a party, something we did quite often and were somewhat noted for, the guest list quickly grew to 34. When Matt arrived I thought we would do a little visiting before telling him how many people were coming. But it wasn't long before we felt very comfortable telling him, and he was delighted. We had the perfect place for the party, a 40'x80' open air pavilion located in the canyon pasture. It was complete with plenty of picnic tables and good cooking arrangements and Matt had everything needed to cater a large party in the back of his truck. With the ease of cooking dinner for two, Matt fed the now close to 40 attendees a variety of food, including quail, shrimp, beef brisket and pork ribs. It was delicious and everyone was amazed at the meal and Matt's engaging personality. What was also amazing was how much work Grant did helping Matt. It was obvious they had done something like this before.

During the course of Matt's first visit, I showed him around the ranch. He absolutely loved it and asked me if I would consider giving him an exclusive hunting lease on the property. He said that he would bring a few people with him each hunting season, and promised that he would not bring anyone that he thought I would object to. I agreed to the arrangement and Matt put together a hunting party every year we were there.

Also, during Matt's first visit, as I showed him around the ranch, I explained to him that we would take our cows to the top of the mesa in the spring and bring them back down in the fall. I told him that we usually had a crew of seven or eight cowboys to help make the drive and that we would feed them breakfast in the morning and dinner at the end of the day, Matt said to call him and let him know when the next drive was going to take place and he would come out and cook for the crew.

That fall when we finalized the plans for bringing the cattle off the mesa, I tried for two days to get in touch with Matt to see if he would like to come out and cook. I finally reached him the afternoon before the drive was to take place at his restaurant in Jefferson, Texas. When I told him the drive was the next day I was surprised when he said he probably could not make it for breakfast, but he would have something ready for the cowboys when they got back down. I really didn't believe he could make the 900 mile drive and have a meal prepared by 2:00 or 3:00 pm the next afternoon.

The next day we had a particularly hard drive. By the time we got back to the bottom everyone was tired and hungry. As we approached the headquarters, I saw Matt's pickup and saw him cooking out of the bed of his truck. By the time we got the horses unsaddled and watered Matt had a four entree meal prepared. Again, we had quail, brisket, shrimp, and the most delicious sugar cured ham you ever tasted.

Matt had driven to Dallas from Jefferson, loaded up his pickup with food and supplies from "No Place" and driven all night to the ranch. This was the kind of friend and companion he was. And, the beauty of it all was that whenever I would call one of the crew to come help me out, they would always ask "Is Matt going to be there to cook", and I would always answer, "I think he might be". I never had a problem getting help.

Matt and Estella came to the ranch many times, usually, as he would say,"just to get back into the woods, drink some Jack Daniels and cook".

Virginia and I looked forward to every one of his visits and each time hated to see him leave. Matt died last year, and we sure miss him.

I Backed Her
Off The Mountain

THIS IS A STORY ABOUT a mare that, because of her agility, smarts and heart, saved my life. Her name was Roxie and she was coal black except for a white star and a few brown hairs in her ears and around her muzzle. She was a full sister to two stakes winners and when she was born we had high hopes for her on the Quarter Horse racing circuit. She was beautiful with perfect confirmation except for her knees, which were offset enough to prevent her from racing. There was no question in my mind that if we had started her as a two or even a three year old she would have broken down. However, with her breeding we knew that she would make a terrific broodmare.

With this in mind we chose the best race bred stud we could afford and took her to be bred in her two year old year. We knew she was very high strung but did not think this trait would have any bearing on her ability to produce quality offspring. We delivered her to the stud farm in late January. For racing purposes, we wanted the foal to be born early the next year.

We received periodic reports from the stud farm during February and March but they were not good. Roxie was not in foal and the attending veterinarian was worried about her condition. She had not adjusted to being away from home and being penned up in a stall and small run. She spent her time pacing the fence and even though the farm was feeding her well she was losing weight. We decided that we would pick her up after her next breeding cycle and if she wasn't in foal we would try again the next year. Sure enough she was not in foal. We had her checked by our vet and he did not find anything wrong with her reproductive system, and could not see why she couldn't get in foal. The next January we took her back to the same stud, and again, she was so uncomfortable at the farm she did not conceive.

So now we had a beautiful race bred mare that we couldn't race and couldn't get in foal.

At the beginning of Roxie's five year old year we decided that even though her knees were offset they probably had matured enough that we could break her and use her as a ranch horse. I figured that her knees would hold up under normal ranch work as opposed to the hard pounding they would have received on the track.

Even though she was high strung she was easy to break and it was evident she enjoyed the work she was being trained to do. She was extremely intelligent and had a natural instinct for working cattle. There was absolutely no indication that her edgy temperament would interfere with her work.

In the two years we used her on the Colorado ranch she did everything that was asked of her. She was definitely a horse you could count on regardless of the task and regardless of the conditions.

Our ranch in Colorado was located on the high plains in Eastern Colorado. It had a beautiful creek running through it and from the creek the land rose on gently rolling hills from an altitude of 5,300 feet at the creek to 6,400 feet at its highest point. Even though there were gullies and washouts that had to be negotiated when looking for and rounding up cattle, it was nothing like the ranch we moved to in New Mexico.

In New Mexico, there were sheer canyon walls that dropped off over 100 feet. The top of Mesa Redonda, where we summered our cows, consisted of just over 4,000 acres, and we did not have or need a fence to keep the cattle on top. The drop-offs around the edge of the mesa were sufficient to keep them from straying off. There was one trail leading to the top that was very steep and narrow. Close to the top, the trail narrowed to about 25 feet where we had a gate across the trail and that was all that was necessary to keep the cattle on their summer pasture.

The mesa was not the only part of the ranch that was rough. There were hills, mini-mesas and ravines, covered with cedar trees that were almost impossible to negotiate. This was especially true of our canyon pasture that led to the trail going to the top of the mesa. It had sheer canyon walls on both sides and a series of cedar covered hills and mini-mesas running along the valley floor.

When it was time to move the cows to the top of the mesa, we would round them up the day before and push them into the canyon pasture. Very early the next morning we would start the drive to the top. The cows and calves would still be fairly close together on the canyon floor and it was relatively easy to gather them to begin the drive.

The Canyon Pasture

On one occasion, however, a storm moved in during the night after we had put the cattle in the canyon pasture. It continued to rain all that night and the next day. We canceled the drive to the top, not only because of the miserable conditions, but because of the treacherous footing on the rain soaked steep trail. Four days later we were finally able to attempt the trip up but we found that the cattle were not concentrated on the canyon floor but were scattered everywhere in the pasture including the sides of the hills and on top of the mini-mesas. We worked most of the morning and thought we had them all gathered, and began pushing them up the trail. As we were going up one cowboy looked back and saw five or six head that we had missed, grazing on top of one of the mesas. K. L. Johnson, one of the best cowboys I had ever worked with, and I went back to get the left behind cows.

We got to the bottom of the little mesa and looked up. We could not see how those cows had climbed up the side of that hill. The mesa was probably 80 feet tall and the sides were extremely steep and wherever there was a possible trail up it was covered with thick cedar trees and bushes. We circled the hill and found a little opening and started up. I was riding Roxie and trusted her surefootedness and willingness to go wherever I wanted her to go. K. L. was in front of me and we began working our way slowly toward the top. We had to crisscross back and forth along the side of the hill pushing our way through the cedars and lunging upward wherever there was a little opening.

We got about 20 feet from the top and were on a very narrow ledge that paralleled the side of the hill. Here we were stuck. We couldn't see any way to the top. K. L. began to edge his horse forward along the ledge looking for some way to keep going up. I turned in my saddle looking over my shoulder to see if there was some sort of opening behind us. I saw a possible cut that I thought could be negotiated and made one of the most stupid moves I had ever made. I turned Roxie toward the side of the mountain. Because the ledge was so narrow, as Roxie tried to turn around, her back feet slid off the edge. Somehow she was able to dig her hoofs into the side of the hill but in doing so was falling over backwards. In a giant effort she was able to turn her body around so that she was now heading straight down. All I could do, as she plunged downward, was hang on. Remarkably Roxie was able to dodge the big cedar trees and crash through the little ones and somehow keep her footing. Almost as remarkable, I was able to stay on until we reached the bottom. I was shaking when I got off her back to see if she was okay. I checked her over and aside from a few scratches on her chest and shoulders she seemed to be in good shape. As for me, I had a few cuts and bruises but was alive.

K. L. carefully worked his way down to where Roxie and I had landed. He asked if I was okay and then said, "You know Boss, I sure thought we had lost you for good." All I could say was, "You know, I backed this mare off the side of the mountain, and if it wasn't for her you would have lost me."

We then made the decision that we should have made in the first place. Leave the dumb cows where they were and push the rest of the herd, including their calves to the top.

As soon as they realized their calves were not close by, they would start looking for them. We pushed the herd on up and back to the water hole on the far end of the mesa. On the way back down off the mesa, I left the gate across the trail open so that our left behind cows could go on up to their calves. Sure enough, about halfway down we passed six cows hurrying up the trail. Their bags were tight and, if nothing else, they were looking for some relief.

When I got back to the barn that night, even though it was late and I was very tired, I put extra bedding in a stall for Roxie and gave her an extra helping of grain. As I turned out the lights in the barn I turned and said, "Thanks, old girl".

People You Can Count On

WHEN YOU ARE IN THE ranching business you very often find yourself in situations where you need help that you know you can count on. This was true of the "over the hill gang" that made up most of my regular crew in New Mexico that helped me with roundups, brandings, shipping and whenever extra help was needed.

It was also true of my family. My wife, Virginia, was always there when I needed her, doing a good job in spite of the impossible situations I put her in. My two daughters, Myka and Jamie, who were such good hands that very often I did not need any other help to get a particularly difficult task done. Then, there was Pat, Myka's husband, who could do anything and always took on far more than his share of the work. I don't know how many times Pat and I worked cattle together, but I cannot think of one time that it didn't turn out the way I hoped.

One spring at the New Mexico ranch it was branding time and I put together my usual crew to gather the cows and calves out of three pastures and put them in one small holding pasture near the headquarters. This pasture had not been grazed so there was plenty of feed for the herd for the three or four days until we finished branding.

I assigned three members of the crew, Don Hofman, retired general manager for the Bell Ranch; Frank Robinson, retired U.S. Navy, and Don McKinley, retired cowboy, to the middle pasture which was the roughest and most difficult pasture to gather. According to my last count there were 78 cows and calves in that pasture. We started about 5:00 in the morning and by noon all the cows, except those in the middle pasture, were already in the holding pen. I was headed for the middle pasture to find out what was going on, when I saw the herd coming down the lane. I went back and opened the gate to let the cows go through. As they went through the gate I counted them and there were only 76 cows and 76 calves. I then saw that Frank was the only one trailing the cattle. When he got to the gate I said "according to my count you are two pair short and it also looks like you are missing two cowboys". Frank agreed and said that there were two wild cows and their calves that had not cooperated and had refused to join the group. The extremely rough country had allowed them to escape several times. Frank said that Hofman and McKinley were still chasing them, determined to bring them in.

I, along with the rest of the crew, went about counting the cows in the holding area and trying to determine if they all had a calf. This took a couple of hours and Hofman and McKinley still had not shown up. I was a little bit worried about my two missing cowboys and decided to go looking for them. As I was cinching up my saddle I saw them coming in on two spent horses. They did not have the two pairs with them and it was easy to see they were pretty dejected. Good cowboys don't like to come in empty handed. I asked Hofman what happened and he said he had been around a lot of cows in his life but he had seldom seen two cows that were wilder than these. He said the last he had seen of them was when they broke through the fence going into the south pasture. He apologized and said they had to give up the chase because their horses were completely worn out. I told him not to worry, that we would find a way to gather them some other time. I didn't think they were going anywhere, but if they did, good riddance.

The Middle pasture

Over the next couple of days we got all of the cows and calves worked. Pat and Myka and their two boys had come down from Colorado to help with the cow work. The day after we finished branding, the whole family went on a ride to explore a rock formation in the south pasture. As we approached the fence line dividing the middle and south pastures we spotted the two cows and calves. They were in the south pasture standing close to a gate on the fence line. I motioned for everyone to stay back and very slowly rode toward the gate. I opened it and rode back to where everyone was waiting. My thought was, and I told Pat, that if we could just get them back into the middle pasture we would be one step closer to gathering them.

We waited at a distance, not moving, for about 30 minutes. One of the cows, followed by her calf, very hesitantly started in the direction of the gate. As she approached the gate the other cow and calf followed. My hope was that if they would go through the gate and far enough from it, I could ride up quickly and shut it. When they were about 30 feet through the gate, I spurred Roxie and made a mad dash to get between them and the fence. When I did, the two pair headed due west toward the highway that bordered the ranch on the west side. Since they were headed that way, I thought that, just maybe, I could hustle them to the fence that ran along the highway and push them all the way back to the headquarters. I was able to get them to the highway fence and turn them north. I thought that if I could stay about 50 feet off of the fence and about 20 feet behind them, I could keep them along the fence for the mile or so it was to the headquarters.

The problem was that when they turned north along the highway their wildest tendencies returned. They broke into a full run. I didn't think that two fat cows with three month old claves could run so fast. It was all that Roxie could do to keep up with them. To complicate matters, this was the roughest part of one of our roughest pastures. The only smooth part was along the highway fence where the cows were. The ground that Roxie and I had to cover was treacherous with steep drop-offs into ravines, deep narrow cuts that had to be jumped and mesquite bushes that had to be avoided. Roxie was going at breakneck speed to stay up with the cows that had the advantage of the fairly smooth terrain along the fence. The only saving grace was that Roxie and I were familiar with the country and this helped us keep up with the stampeding cows.

When we got about a quarter of a mile from the east-west fence at the headquarters, I said to myself, "What the hell am I going to do now?" There was not a gate, much less an open gate, that I could push them through. The nearest gate was a quarter-mile along the fence to the east and it was not open. I was about to quit the chase, thinking that I could not possibly keep them on the fence and at the same time get ahead of them to open the gate when I heard something behind me. I turned around in my saddle and saw ever dependable Pat about a hundred feet back. This was a complete surprise because I had not in any way communicated to him what I was attempting to do. But, when he realized what I was trying to do, he covered the rough country in record time. I slowed down a bit to let Pat catch up with me and pointed to the East and yelled for him to cut across and open the gate going into the horse pasture. Pat knew exactly what I wanted and he did it.

When the cows got to the fence at the headquarters they were pretty tired. I was able to get them headed east down that fence line to what I hoped would be an open gate into the horse pasture. As we proceeded east they got their wind back and again started to run. As fast as they were running I really didn't think it would be possible to turn them through any open gate, if there was one. As we approached where the gate was I could see that it was open and Pat had positioned himself perfectly to allow the cows to see the opening and encourage them to go through it. When they got to the gate they turned through it like there was no other place to go.

I rode up to Pat as he was closing the gate behind the cows and I said, "You know, there was a lot of luck involved in what we were able to do today, but it seems to me that every time we work cattle together we get the job done." He agreed.

All of this happened on a Thursday, and the next day, I did two things. First, I called Don Hofman and told him that Pat and I were able to get done what he and super cowboy Don McKinley were unable to do, and second, I took the two cows and their calves to the sale at Dalhart. I really enjoyed doing both.

Pat on Ten

The Horse Corral

I REALLY DON'T KNOW HOW OR why I have been so lucky with respect to the horses I have owned and known throughout my ranching days. I don't consider myself an expert horseman like some people I know, but it seems that almost every horse I have been associated with has been special.

Here are some pictures and short comments about a few of them. This is nowhere near a complete list, nor are the comments an adequate description of the character or traits of those mentioned, but I hope the reader will come away with some idea of how good they were in what they did. They were very much a part of mine and my family's life.

Lusty Lu

Lusty deserves more attention and space because he was not just something special, he was super special. It was only by happenstance that we acquired Lusty. Virginia and I were at a race bred horse sale in Oklahoma City with the intention of purchasing a good brood mare. The sale was a three day event and we looked over the prospects and selected two or three mares to bid on.

As we were going through the barns looking at the horses for sale, a yearling colt caught our eye. This was not what we needed but Virginia kept dragging me back to his stall, and I knew that I was in trouble. On the second day of the sale we bought one of the mares we were looking at and decided to return home. The colt had not yet gone through the ring and Virginia begged me to stay and bid on him. We didn't have any money left to buy another horse but in order to get her in the truck to drive back to Colorado, I promised her that if the colt did not sell when it went through the ring, I would contact the owner and see if we could make a deal. On the twelve hour drive back to our ranch, Virginia kept pointing out the good features of the colt, and convinced me that I needed to follow up on my promise.

The next day I called the sale barn and asked if the colt had sold and was told that the owner had "no saled" him. I contacted the owner and we agreed upon a price. I said that I would pick the colt up the next day. I thought I would go by myself, but Virginia was so excited she had to go along with me. We brought him home and from that moment on I was eternally grateful to Virginia for insisting that we get him.

We had so many good experiences with Lusty and so many stories that I could write a complete book just about him. But, there is one important lesson that I would like to include here. It's about Lusty's breeding and what I learned from it.

Lusty was by Triple Lu, a prominent Thoroughbred stallion, and out of a Quarter Horse mare that was sired by a horse named Wilson Yellow Cat. I was not familiar with Wilson Yellow Cat but I was very impressed with Triple Lu, both as a race horse and as a sire. As Lusty matured and became everything you could ever want in a horse, I started looking for another horse sired by Triple Lu that might be somewhat comparable to Lusty. I had been told all my life that the pedigree of the dam was just as important, if not more so, than the pedigree of the sire, but I forgot this, and concentrated exclusively on trying to find some offspring of Triple Lu that might fill the bill.

Within reason, I went to every sale that had a colt or filly in it sired by Triple Lu. I was determined to find another Lusty. If having one was good, having two would be better. After traveling many miles and looking at several prospects, I was disappointed and discouraged. None of them seemed to have the confirmation or glint in the eye that Virginia and I had seen in Lusty. As time went on I abandoned my efforts to find what I was looking for.

A couple of years passed and a friend gave me his collection of American Quarter Horse Association Journals, which dated back to the founding of AQHA. I started going through them reading the articles about the foundation sires and mares and looking at the advertisements for Stallions that were standing at the time. I came across an advertisement for a stud by the name of Wilson Yellow Cat. I was taken aback, because the picture of him looked exactly like

Lusty, as did the pictures of his prodigy that were included in the ad. All of these years I had been looking at the offspring of Triple Lu, when I should have been looking at the offspring of Wilson Yellow Cat. The ad in the journal was several years old and I was not able to find any mares by Wilson Yellow Cat that I could pick up, so I was never able to come close to duplicating Lusty. But this lesson served me well in the years ahead. In evaluating a horse that I intended to purchase, or breed a mare to, the bloodlines of the dam were of utmost importance.

Frosty and Lil' Buck

Frosty and Buck were Myka's and Jamie's first horses. When we moved to the ranch in Colorado, the first order of business was to find them each a good horse. They both knew how to ride, and even though they were both young they needed more than just a kid pony.

I took three days and went to every ranch, horse trading operation, auction barn, etc. that advertised what I considered might make a good first horse for the two of them. I wanted their first experience with a horse of their own to be a good experience. During my three day search, I must have tried 40 horses and, as I alluded to earlier, I was extremely lucky. The horses I selected turned out to be perfect.

I decided on Frosty for Myka, a palomino colored Appaloosa mare that could and did everything Myka asked of her. She took care of Myka and helped her develop into the excellent horse woman she is today.

Buck was the best possible horse for Jamie. He was only fourteen hands tall, but was all horse. He taught Jamie the meaning of competition and the two of them became a winning team.

Roxie

All you have to do is read the story "I Backed Her off the Mountain" to know how I felt about this magnificent mare. As I said in the story, that even though she was a very well bred race mare with two stakes winning brothers, we could not run her because she had two slightly offset knees. Also, in the story, I explained our unsuccessful efforts to breed her when she was a young filly. So, because we couldn't run her or get her in foal, we broke her and trained her as a working cow horse, and next to Lusty, she was the best I ever owned.

It was because of her natural ability and determination that we finally had to put her down. When working cattle, whether trailing or sorting them, anticipation and positioning are of upmost importance. Roxie was one of the best, she anticipated a cow's every move and was always in the right place to head it off and turn it back, but this required quick maneuvers that were hard on the legs.

I was helping a friend gather a large pasture in New Mexico and was riding Roxie. This ranch was about fifty miles from our ranch at Mesa Redonda, and I was not familiar with the country. We rounded up the cows and were pushing them back to the corrals at the headquarters. It was a very hot day and the cows couldn't understand why it was necessary that they be moved on this particular day. One or two of them were always trying to break away from the herd, so we had to be constantly alert to what they might do. Roxie would sense a problem and instantly move to keep any would be strays in line. This usually meant a mad dash to head them off and turn them back to the herd.

Things were going okay until we came upon about a mile stretch of push sand. Going through this soft, fine sand was hard on both the cattle and the horses. The cattle got cranky and it became harder and harder to keep them together and push them on. Roxie was constantly going from one side of the herd to the other to make sure we didn't lose any. Because she was the best horse on this drive the burden fell heaviest on her. By the time we got through the sand and the cattle penned, she was tired and I could tell she was hurting. On the drive back to Mesa Redonda, all I could think about was what effect the day's work had on those bad knees. When we got to the ranch I rubbed her front legs with liniment and put her into a heavily bedded stall.

The next morning when I checked on her, my worst fears became a reality. Her knees were twice their normal size, and she could barely walk. Over the next few weeks, I kept her on butazolidin and did everything I could to keep her comfortable. She gradually got better, but I knew that she would never be able to work again. I also knew that she had a home for as long as she lived.

As she improved I thought about trying to breed her again but I didn't want to put her through the stress she had experienced when we had tried before. Jamie, through a friend, found a pretty good race bred stallion that was being used as a remuda sire on a large ranch near Tucumcari. The stallion was used to pasture breed about twenty mares a year and I thought that Roxie might settle in with the mares and not be so stressed. I looked at some of the stallion's offspring and liked what I saw. This was in late February and I waited until she showed signs of coming into heat and took her to the ranch. I dropped her off in the pasture and waited to see how she was going to get along with her new suitor and his band of mares. After awhile it was apparent that she was going to fit in, and I said to myself, "You know this may just work". It did, her first foal was a beautiful sorrel colt that we named "Stinky". Soon after Stinky was born we decided to take her back to rebreed her to the same stud. It worked again, and her second foal was a sorrel filly that was almost identical in color and confirmation to "Stinky". We named her "Sis" after my Mother who had recently passed away. Stinky went on to win five out of eight races on the bush tracks in New Mexico, and Sis won four out of seven on the bush tracks in Texas.

After Sis was born it became apparent that Roxie was near her end. She could barely get around and was obviously in pain. We kept her on butazolidin and did everything we could to keep her comfortable. When Sis was weaned I decided that it would be best to put her down. It was a very hard decision, one that I think about quite often.

Lucky

Lucky was the most "bullet proof" horse I have ever known. By bullet proof I mean that you could count on him to never do anything unpredictable. It seemed as if his main goal in life was to take care of the person on his back.

Virginia bought Lucky from the previous owner of our New Mexico ranch who said that he knew every inch of the treacherous terrain on, in and around Mesa Redonda. Virginia had ridden Lucky a couple of times and felt very comfortable with him, and decided that he would be the perfect horse for her.

We paid a lot of money for Lucky and at the time I thought it was way too much. But, as it turned out, it wasn't. He never took a bad step and Virginia felt safe riding him and I felt safe having her on him. That, in and of itself, is worth a lot.

I rode Lucky working cows almost as much as I did Roxie, and he never let me down. I was chasing a wild cow one day and I sort of had her boxed into the end of a little ravine. I was waiting for some help from other members of the crew, and was trying to keep still so as not to spook the cow, when I heard the distinct buzzing sound of a large rattlesnake. I knew it was close, but I didn't know how close. My first thought was, that Lucky was probably going to jump out from under me and leave me on top of or near the snake. But, no thanks to me, he remained perfectly calm and quiet.

I gasped for air and looked around to see if I could locate what I hoped was only a bad dream. I finally saw the snake, about a foot in front of Lucky's front feet, coiled and ready to strike. In a very quiet, shaky voice, I said to Lucky, "This is it ol' boy, let's just back out of here a few feet and we will be okay." I gave a slight tug on the reins and Lucky, step by step, slowly backed up out of the snake's striking range. I turned him around and we moved off a few more feet. I got off and checked Lucky to make sure the snake had not struck him before I had known it was there. He was okay and couple of hours later I was okay also.

You know, I don't remember what happened with the cow.

Winter fun in Colorado, Lil' Buck pulling a sled

Jamie and Lusty winning Cow Pony Race

Author and Roxie packing a deer out of Canyon pasture

Roxie's colt Stinky

Roxie's filly Sis winning on East Texas bush track

Virginia and Lucky in East pasture

Epilogue

Over the years that I was engaged in ranching I thought about the many wonderful experiences that I had. They were not unique to me as most ranchers have had or suffered the same type of happenings. I did not expect to put anything down in writing, but I often thought about the experiences and realized how much I enjoyed reliving them. Then one day I sat down and put pen to paper and wrote the first of the stories, " It Doesn't Get Any Better Than This", and thought to myself that I would like everyone to know what all of this meant to me and hope that some of the readers would come away with the same feelings. Clint Hoagland was a very special friend. We worked hard together and played hard together, and getting the best of one another was a constant goal. After drafting that first story I decided that there were other stories that were worth telling, about my family, other friends and the horses and dogs that were a part of my everyday life. And, most of all, it was how I felt about the land on which I ranched. Whenever I thought about the land, it evoked a lot of emotion.

I consider myself so fortunate to have lived on some of

the most beautiful land in this country. Our ranch in Colorado was on the East Bijou Creek which was lined with huge two hundred year old Cottonwood trees that were truly magnificent. From the creek the land rose to the high plains, gently rolling hills that were cut by deep washouts and canyons. The grass on those hills and in the valleys was short, thick and nutritious. A friend, who was also my mentor, and I ran yearlings over about 5000 to 8000 acres for several years. My uncle, who graduated from Texas A&M in animal husbandry, would come to Colorado from East Texas about every year, and seeing how fat and healthy our yearlings were, was amazed at how well they were doing on nothing but the short buffalo and gramma grass. It was a beautiful country and a wonderful experience.

A lot of people, who were a lot smarter than me, especially in the area of making money, encouraged me to subdivide our ranch and capitalize on the encroaching population from Denver and Colorado Springs. I could not bring myself to do that but my neighbor did, he divided the land around us and pretty soon we had a lot of new neighbors.

We sold out and bought the New Mexico ranch. It was high desert country and Mesa Redonda, which rose to over 1500 feet from the base, was unbelievable. Again, I could not believe how fortunate I was to own this piece of land. Generally, I do not care to go horseback riding, for the sake of riding a horse. If there was not a specific purpose for riding, such as rounding up cattle or roping and branding, I was not particularly interested. But, on the ranch in New Mexico

I rode just to explore the country and take in its beauty. We sold the ranch because of a severe five-year drought, and Virginia wanted to return to East Texas to be with her mother.

I have often lamented and felt sorry for myself for having to move off of these two beautiful ranches. Whenever I did I would also think what it must have been like when, in 1830, Congress passed the Indian Removal Act to forcibly relocate the Cherokee from their beloved hills and fertile farm lands in Georgia to lands west of the Mississippi; when the Apache were removed from their beautiful mountains in western New Mexico and eastern Arizona and shipped in cattle cars to distant Florida; when the Comanche saw their entire horse herds slaughtered so they could be defeated and relocated from the Mesa Redonda and Palo Dura Canyon country to Oklahoma; when the Southern Cheyenne and Kiowa were killed at Sand Creek in eastern Colorado, having been driven from the East Bijou Creek valley; when the sacred Black Hills were taken from the Sioux because gold had been discovered in their mountains; and when the Nez Perce were chased from their ancestral home, the beautiful valley of winding water in Oregon.

Chief Joseph, describing his father's death: "I buried him in that beautiful valley of winding water. I love that land more than all the rest of the world".

I think I know how they felt.

CPSIA information can be obtained at www.ICGtesting.com
Printed in the USA
LVOW060516170512

282057LV00001B/5/P